LOCAL GOVERNMENT IN ANCIENT INDIA

LOCAL GOVERNMENT IN ANCIENT INDIA

RADHAKUMUD MOOKERJI, M.A., Ph.D.

GYAN

Published by

GYAN

Gyan Publishing House
5, Ansari Road
Daryaganj, New Delhi-110002
Phone: 011-47034999, 9811692060
E-mail: books@gyanbooks.com

Distribution Network
gyanbooks.com
India, USA, Canada, UK, Australia, France

ISBN : 978-81-212-9532-1 (PB)
First Published, 1919

2nd Impression 2023

Printed at: Gyan Press, Delhi.

LOCAL GOVERNMENT IN ANCIENT INDIA
Author: RADHAKUMUD MOOKERJI

MYSORE UNIVERSITY STUDIES

HISTORICAL SERIES: No. I.

By the same Author

1. A HISTORY OF INDIAN SHIPPING AND MARITIME ACTIVITY from the Earliest Times. (Longmans.) 7s. 6d. net.

2. THE FUNDAMENTAL UNITY OF INDIA (from Hindu Sources). (Longmans.) 3s. 6d. net.

3. AN INTRODUCTION TO INDIAN ECONOMICS. (Calcutta.)

4. THE EDUCATIONAL ORGANIZATION OF ANCIENT INDIA. [*In preparation.*

5. STUDIES IN ANCIENT INDIAN HISTORY. [*In the press.*

6. THE EMPIRE OF CHANDRAGUPTA MAURYA. [*In preparation.*

LOCAL GOVERNMENT IN ANCIENT INDIA

BY

RADHAKUMUD MOOKERJI, M.A., PH.D.

VIDYAVAIBHAVA

Premchand Roychand Scholar, Calcutta University;
Professor of History, and Fellow, Mysore University;
Member of the Benares Hindu University Court;
Sometime Manindra Professor of Ancient Indian History in the Benares Hindu University;
Author of
'A History of Indian Shipping',
'The Fundamental Unity of India (from Hindu Sources)', &c.

1919

TO

HIS HIGHNESS

SRI KRISHNA RAJA WADIYAR BAHADUR

G.C.S.I., G.B.E.,

MAHARAJA OF MYSORE

FOUNDER AND CHANCELLOR OF MYSORE UNIVERSITY

CHANCELLOR OF BENARES UNIVERSITY

WHO REPRESENTS THE BEST IDEALS OF A HINDU KING

AND

WHOSE NAME IS A HOUSEHOLD WORD THROUGHOUT INDIA

FOR HIS

MATCHLESS MUNIFICENCE IN THE CAUSE OF LEARNING

AUTHOR'S PREFACE

THE present work aims at a systematic presentation of an important aspect of Indian culture-history, the origin and development of various local institutions through which the communal life of the country expressed itself. The remarkable range, volume, and variety of the evidence bearing on the subject call for a methodical and scientific treatment which will bring into prominence the exuberant vitality and manifold growth of self-governing institutions among a people characterized by a genius for social experiments and constructions.

The treatment of the evidence as a connected and comprehensive whole is, however, not free from certain difficulties owing to its special character. This has been discussed in the work towards the conclusion. The evidence of the North and the evidence of the South are separated, for example, not merely by a distance in space, but also by a distance in time. The later date of the southern evidence has been explained by a competent archaeologist on the assumption that the institutions referred to therein were importations from the

North, and hence late in their appearance in the South. Both the evidences point, in fact, to parallel lines of development with the necessary local variations. The substantial similarity of the organizations in the North and the South has been the main argument in favour of subjecting them to a common treatment. Intensive studies of local areas have been sometimes supposed to be the only admissible method for investigating the social phenomena of a country like India possessed of such vast territorial extent and variety of social stratification and composition, but, in the majority of cases, such studies do not weaken, but strengthen, the case for generalizations and extensive studies for the whole of India. Sometimes, local developments are indeed better understood as parts of a wider and more fundamental one: a study of the whole throws light on the parts. The truth is that India is fundamentally one, physically and culturally. I have very often found that the literary and epigraphic evidence, the law-books and the inscriptions, support and explain one another in spite of their differences in date and locality.

In this connexion I may indicate two possible sources of error in historical treatment. The first is to lose sight of the organic inter-connexions of cultural developments in the mass of local particulars. This naturally leads to a narrow sectional view of

Indian history that seeks, for example, to pit Aryan against non-Aryan, South against North, Brahmanical records and sources against Buddhist, or indigenous growths, evolutions, and assimilations against foreign importations, imitations, or exploitations. The second is to miss the spontaneity and significance of specific variations which give body and shape to the generic experiences of the historical consciousness in particular environments. This has been a fruitful source of historic misinterpretations, among which we may mention the tendency to see in Indian history endless repetitions of one invariable type of state and political institutions, autocratic and theocratic in their character, thus to apply the linear view of social evolution to Indian political developments; or to interpret the various indigenous codes of law as being based only on the rigid concept of sovereignty without recognizing how largely are the origins of law and constitution in India traceable to the pristine factors of the indigenous scheme of social values.

Here I may as well raise a caveat against certain sources of bias which are apt to vitiate our historical judgements. Sometimes there is an unfounded belief in immobile, exaggerated racial types, in an exclusive European or Asiatic mentality, which, if true, would make Indian history disparate with European. Others again have sought to interpret and appraise Indian culture in terms of the fundamental concepts of Western social progress and civilization. This unfortunately amounts to putting Indian life in all its original and spontaneous forms and vigorous growths into the Procrustean bed of the shibboleths and copy-book maxims of Western social science. I have tried my best to be on my guard against these sources of bias. If I have occasionally seemed to be guilty of reading into ancient records the modern notions of the West, perhaps the very conditions of writing on indigenous topics in a foreign language are largely responsible for it. I have been driven to the necessity of using, for instance, such familiar terms of Western political experience as guilds (craft-guilds and merchant-guilds), partnerships, municipalities, and the like, but they do not always imply precisely corresponding institutions in Indian politics with an exact identity of structure and functions. I have used them in a broad sense as convenient symbols to express allied realities or notions. It will also, I trust, be found that I have not made any observations or drawn any conclusions which are not supported by the clearest texts or other adequate evidence.

Finally, it has to be borne in mind that the methods of investigation as well as canons of criticism which apply to the social sciences, or studies in culture-history, must differ from those of the physical sciences which deal with phenomena admitting of exact quantitative measurement.

There are a few minor points to which I may also advert in this connexion. In the introduction I have put forward, as a tentative suggestion, the hypothesis about the peculiar relations between the state and society in ancient India which has, to my mind, the merit of explaining some of the paradoxes in its history and throwing light on some of its obscure aspects or chapters. The introduction, I trust, will thus be found to be a contribution to the study of Indian political evolution. Another point requiring mention is that in citing South Indian evidence I have had reasons to depart from the chronological limits of the ancient period of Indian history, and to bring within its purview certain passages of what is generally regarded as the mediaeval period of that history. For it has to be recognized that there are certain fundamental factors which do not always permit the ancient and mediaeval periods of North and South Indian history to agree closely in chronological limits. There are wide divergences in the dates of our evidence in the North and the South, and, consequently, in the dates of the corresponding historical developments, so that to apply under such dissimilar circumstances a common chronological criterion would be an attempt at a forced and artificial uniformity. The ancient period is longer in the South than in the North, while the mediaeval period may be regarded as dating practically from the battle of Talikota (A. D. 1565), the date of the downfall of the great Hindu Empire of Vijayanagara, the last of the independent political states of ancient Hindu India.[1] Accordingly, there are numerous references in the work to South Indian evidence, ranging in dates from the ninth to the twelfth and even thirteenth and fourteenth centuries A. C., while the evidence for the North closes at a much earlier period. The third point requiring notice is that, while the evidence of the South Indian inscriptions is copious in its details respecting the constitution of the local bodies, that of the North is practically devoid of such details, which can only be but partially gathered from the literary texts. As regards the terms used for such local bodies, the South Indian inscriptions invariably use two terms, viz. *Mahāsabhā* and *Sabhā*, indicating respectively the general or the greater assembly and the smaller and subordinate committee of the larger body, while the corresponding terms used in the northern inscriptions are *Śreṇī*, *Nigama*, and *Nigama-Sabhā*. It may be noted in passing that the use of Sanskrit

[1] It may be noted that the treatment of South Indian history in the *Imperial Gazetteer*, new ed., adopts the same chronological limit.

terms for these local bodies in the South is one more indication of the fact that they are parts of a common Indian system with organic affinities. The last point on which I should like to comment is that the present work does not treat of all classes of local bodies in ancient India: the educational and purely religious bodies, like the *pariṣads* and *saṅghas* for instance, which require separate monographs by themselves, have been excluded from its purview. I have already announced a monograph on 'Educational Institutions in Ancient India'.

Portions of the book were formed into a paper which I read before a meeting of the Mythic Society, Bangalore, under the presidency of the Hon. Mr. Cobb, the British Resident of Mysore, February, 1918. The paper was published in the following April issue of the *Journal of the Mythic Society*.

I owe special acknowledgements to the Marquess of Crewe, K.G., for his Foreword, to Dr. Brajendranath Seal, M.A., Ph.D., George V Professor of Philosophy in the Calcutta University, for some very valuable improvements, and to Mr. V. A. Smith, M.A., the learned historian, for his kind interest in my work shown by seeing it through the Press. I am also thankful to my colleague, Mr. M. Hiriyanna, M.A., the University Professor of Sanskrit, for his revision of the work and several valuable suggestions.

I am profoundly grateful to His Highness the Maharaja of Mysore for his gracious permission to dedicate to him, the Founder and Chancellor of the Mysore University, this humble work.

RADHAKUMUD MOOKERJI.

MYSORE UNIVERSITY,
MYSORE,
September 10, 1918.

CONTENTS

INTRODUCTION

§ I.

ONE of the characteristic features of ancient Hindu civilization is the marked development of associated life it exhibits. That development was achieved in varying degrees in the different spheres of life. We find it in those of religion, learning, politics, civics, and economics. In all these spheres organizations grew up on what may be regarded as a democratic or popular basis to fulfil the ends of national life. A proper presentation of Hindu culture in all its aspects and phases should take into account these diverse developments of the associated life, the many manifestations of the democratic principle which that culture represents. In the present work an attempt will be made to trace one particular line of that development, to dwell upon the workings of the democratic principle in one particular sphere.

The subject of Local Self-Government in ancient India has both historical and practical interest. We owe largely to her elaborate system of local government the preservation of the integrity, independence, and individuality of Hindu culture, despite the world-shaking and catastrophic political movements to which that culture was frequently exposed in the course of her history. That provided a sort of Noah's ark in which were safely protected the vital elements of Hindu civilization against the overwhelming political deluges that swept over the country from time to time. As Sir George Birdwood has truly remarked: 'India has undergone more religious and political revolutions than any other country in the world; but the village communities remain in full municipal vigour all over the peninsula. Scythian, Greek, Saracen, Afghan, Mongol, and Marātha have come down from its mountains, and Portuguese, Dutch, English, French, and Dane up out of its seas, and set up their successive dominations in the land; but the religious trades-union villages have remained as little affected by their coming and going as a rock by the rising and falling of the tide'.[1] This is indeed an echo of an earlier utterance of Sir Charles Metcalfe: 'The village communities are little republics, having nearly everything they can want within themselves, and almost independent of any foreign relations. They seem to last where nothing else lasts. Dynasty after dynasty tumbles down; revolution succeeds to revolution; . . . but the village community remains the same. . . This

[1] *Industrial Arts of India*, p. 320.

union of the village communities, each one forming a separate little state in itself, has, I conceive, contributed more than any other cause to the preservation of the peoples of India, through all the revolutions and changes which they have suffered, and is in a high degree conducive to their happiness, and to the enjoyment of a great portion of freedom and independence'.[1]

The fact is that India presents the rare and remarkable phenomenon of the state and the society co-existing apart from, and in some degree of independence of each other, as distinct and separate units or entities, as independent centres of national, popular, and collective life and activity. Both of them were independent organisms with distinct and well-defined structures and functions of their own and laws of growth and evolution. The limits of state-interference were accordingly so defined and fixed as not to encroach upon the sphere of the activities of the social organization. A policy of non-interference was recognized as the ideal policy of the state, the functions of which were ordinarily restricted to 'the irreducible minimum', viz. the protection of life and property and realization of the revenue for the proper execution of that duty. There was a well-understood delimitation of the respective

[1] *Rep. Select Comm. of House of Commons*, 1832, vol. III, app. 84, p. 331.

boundaries of the political and the social organization, both of which were co-operating agencies for the promotion of the common weal. This peculiar and predominant tendency in ancient and mediaeval Indian politics is in marked contrast with that of European or Western politics generally. In the West the predominant tendency has been towards a progressive extension of state interference and state control so as to bring within its limits all the main departments of social life and national activity until the ideal is attained of a complete nationalization or socialization of all the means and processes of life itself. The state, beginning as an agent of society, becomes its master and representative; society is merged in the state to which it surrenders its functions, dropping its independent life. Thus in the West the king or the repository of the sovereign power is the head of the state as well as of society, including even the church in some cases. In ancient India the king was head of the state, but not of the society. He had a place in the social hierarchy, but it was not the highest place. As the symbol of the state he appeared to the people like a remote abstraction with no direct touch with their daily life, which was governed by the social organization. The points of contact between the state and the ordinary interests of the daily life of the people were indeed very few.

In bringing out this contrast between the tendencies of Indian and Western politics and political thought it is not meant that Western administrations leave no room for local self-government or have no place for the autonomous local and municipal bodies. The assumption indeed goes against the very nature of things. For it is physically impossible to administer properly the manifold interests of civilized life in the comparatively larger states of the modern world from one central government. Indeed, if we consider the most progressive countries of the West, such as the United Kingdom, Germany, France, or the United States, we shall find that by far the largest part of their government is now that which is not carried on in the capital cities by the dignified departments of state under the control of the Central National Assembly or Parliament, but that which is being administered locally in village, or parish, or commune, in municipality, or county, or district, under the control and in the interests of the local people in these limited areas. In England, for instance, the aggregate of parish councils, district councils, borough councils, and county councils happens to be, in magnitude or volume of business, greater than all the Government Departments put together. In these advanced countries the local bodies between them spend more money, undertake more enterprises, employ more officials, and legislate more extensively than the central government.[1] But, granting all this, it is evident that these organizations of local government are mostly the creation of the central government; that these local bodies owe their present form and constitution to a process of decentralization, delegation, or devolution of powers determined by the national legislature; that they are thus in the ultimate analysis but wheels of a common machine, parts of a single plant, and are not by any means 'extra-legal' associations, devoid of any statutory warrant, and, therefore, in the eye of the law, possessed of no authority whatsoever.[2]

In respect of local self-government as it developed in India, however, we shall find that the Indian institutions are practically *sui generis*, representing a type which may be sharply distinguished from the type represented by the corresponding institutions in modern polity. The fundamental difference is that while, in the latter case, the state, as a fully developed and completely constituted body, consciously creates autonomous centres within

[1] See Sidney Webb's Preface to Dr. John Matthai's *Village Government in British India*, a work to which I owe some valuable suggestions.

[2] It should be borne in mind that in the body of the text reference is made only to modern conditions as they exist in England and other countries of the West. Of course, the writer is aware that in many respects there is a remarkable approximation between early and mediaeval conditions of local government in England and those prevailing in ancient India.

itself by devolution and delimitation of its own functions, in the former the communal institutions, guilds, and local bodies have an independent origin and growth out of fluid and inchoate conditions of tribal life and organization. When the state comes to supervene or be superimposed upon these, it has to treat with them more or less on terms of equality and recognize their pre-existing rights by conventions and agreements which operate as charters regulating their mutual relations. Thus the varied interests of the communal life, such as administrative, judicial, civic, commercial, or industrial, are assured by the voluntary co-operation of independent and integral units of a common body politic.

The foregoing characterization of the system of local government in ancient India and the relations that obtained between state and society as independent organizations and centres of national life will also perhaps help us to explain and account for the somewhat perplexing phenomenon of the rise of the few empires in early Indian history administering vast and varied areas and, on two occasions, a territory more extensive than British India, stretching from Afghanistan to Mysore. It is difficult even to conceive how it was physically possible, in the absence of the modern means and facilities of communication, to control a continent from one centre in an isolated corner of India such as that at Pātaliputra when the news of a disturbance beyond the north-western frontier in central Asia or Arachosia would probably take six months' time to reach the headquarters of government. And yet the growth of such an imperial authority is attested by sober history. It is not sufficiently recognized that India in the olden times was not a land of jungles and wastes, but a land of abundant agriculture, brisk trade, numerous arts and crafts, convenient roads and trade-routes with wells and rest-houses, shade-giving groves and fruit-bearing trees at regular intervals, and prosperous cities. The Greek writers on Alexander's campaigns speak of 2,000 regular towns in the Panjāb alone. But these material factors, though they go a great way, do not by themselves exhaust or constitute that assemblage of conditions which make the governance of empires of such colossal dimensions at all feasible. The fact is that for an adequate explanation of this puzzling phenomenon we have to look beyond the material and the objective, the physical and the natural, to the subjective and the spiritual aspects of the situation. Man's inventiveness is meant to triumph over the difficulties of his natural environment. And so the natural difficulties in the way of the Mauryan empire were solved by human statesmanship, by the the application or evolution of a system of administration giving effect to an extensive decentralization and utmost latitude to the operations of local government, so that numerous autonomous centres were at work to cope with the administrative requirements of an extensive territory. This appropriate administrative machinery was not, however, be it understood, so much the creation of the new empire-builders—and Asoka at least is very careful in distinguishing his *innovations* from his *inheritances*[1]—as a legacy and a heritage handed down to them from older days. They formed an administrative machinery, fairly adequate to its purposes, already in existence and operation, that had stood the test of centuries, the strain of political revolutions, ministering to the normal needs of national life in the deeper strata of society, unaffected by the political currents that disturb the upper strata, or the changes in ruling dynasties, and all the while conserving the vital elements in the culture of the race. It was such a machinery that made the way smooth for the emperors whose task was only to fight their way to the throne, win battles, maintain their power, and adapt the pre-existing administrative institutions to the requirements of the new times with their new problems. The most brilliant of the Indian emperors can be credited with but few administrative innovations. The fact of the matter is that just as the aloofness of society from

[1] See Rock Edict III, VI, VIII, Kalinga R.E. II, P.E. IV, V, &c.

the state has been the main means of its self-preservation when the state is engulfed in political revolutions, and the independent development of local government has provided, like the shell of the tortoise, a haven of peace where the national culture can draw in for its own safety when political storms burst over the land—so also does this system serve to lighten considerably the burden of a new administration, with the result that the addition of mere territory does not materially add to its difficulties. The administration of the Mauryan empire was possible because it did not cherish the ambition of setting up a centralized government consciously legislating for and controlling the life of every part of that vast whole, but aimed only at an elastic system of federalism or confederation in which were incorporated, along with the central government at the metropolis, as parts of the same system, the indigenous local administrations. The essence of this imperial system was thus a recognition of local autonomy at the expense of the authority of the central government, which was physically unfit to assert itself except by its enforced affiliation to the pre-existing system of local government.[1]

[1] The absence of proper physical facilities, factors, or conditions is perhaps one of the reasons why empires in ancient India have been so few and short-lived. The following observations of J. S. Mill [*Representative Government*, p. 4] are very interesting and appropriate on the point: 'In the ancient world, though there might be, and

In the same way, the existence of a system of social self-government in practical independence of the ruling powers and unaffected by the vicissitudes of fortune to which they are naturally exposed will account for the somewhat remarkable fact that, even during the period of so much unrest and unsettlement under the Muhammadan rulers, Hindu India was able to show a good record of material, mental, and moral progress. Hindu India was able to live her usual life, to continue the course of her normal intellectual and spiritual progress, in her own socio-economic system in which the Muhammadan had no place. The alien kings took possession of the political capital, but they had to live in the mere suburbs of the real metropolis of India. In this sense the so-called Muhammadan period of Indian

often was, great individual or local independence, there could be nothing like a regulated popular government, beyond the bounds of a single city-community; because there did not exist the physical conditions for the formation and propagation of a public opinion, except among those who could be brought together to discuss public matters in the same *agora*. . . . There have been states of society in which even a monarchy of any great territorial extent could not subsist, but unavoidably broke up into petty principalities, either mutually independent, or held together by a loose tie like the feudal; because the machinery of authority was not perfect enough to carry orders into effect at a great distance from the person of the ruler. He depended mainly upon voluntary fidelity for the obedience even of his army, nor did there exist the means of making the people pay an amount of taxes sufficient for keeping up the force necessary to compel obedience throughout a large territory.'

history may be regarded as wrongly named, because it continued to be a period of the usual Hindu activity, the normal course of which was hardly interrupted by the political changes of the times, which were nothing new to Indian history. The culture of the race kept up its uninterrupted flow, as is evident from the many intellectual and religious movements, and the appearance of many great men in the realms of both thought and action which characterize the period.

In the eighth century we have the great Brahman preacher and reformer Kumārila, who recalled the people to the simpler Vedic religious rites and ceremonies in the midst of the confusion and corruptions of numerous sects. The ninth century is famous for another gift of South India, Sankarāchāryya, the profound Sanskrit scholar and writer, an eloquent preacher and a great religious reformer and organizer, who travelled throughout India in pursuit of his spiritual *digvijaya*, and imparted to Hinduism that broad philosophical basis and certain new elements which helped it to establish itself once again as the dominant and popular religion of India. The ascendancy of the Rajputs then followed in the later centuries, which meant an accession of strength to Hinduism, as is evident from the multiplicity of sects and the sectarian controversies of the times, producing a crop of religious and philosophical literary works composed generally in Sanskrit, of which the most numerous were those written by the Saiva worshippers of Kashmīr. The intellectual history of those centuries is represented by such famous names as Bhavabhūti, a member of the court, first of Yasovarman of Kanauj and afterwards of Lalitāditya (A. D. 730); Magha (A. D. 800); Padmagupta (A. D. 950); Srī Harsha, the author of Naiṣadha (A. D. 1150), and courtier of Jayachandra of Kanauj, Bhatta-Nārāyana (A. D. 850), of the Pāla court of Bihar; Rājaśekhara (A. D. 900) of the Tomara court of Kanauj; Jayadeva (A. D. 1100) and the Kashmīrian poets Somadeva, Kshemendra, and Bilhana of the twelfth century; and the chronicler Kalhana, author of the *Rājatarangini*. In the eleventh century Southern India witnessed the great Lingāyat revival under Basava, and in the twelfth the Vaisnavite revival under Rāmānuja, followed by the great Brahmana teacher of the Kanarese country, Mādhava Pūrṇaprajña, who died towards the close of the same century. Later on, a fresh instance of Hindu vitality is found in the growth of the Vijayanagara empire, which was at once a centre of both political and literary life, as represented by the famous Sāyanāchāryya and his school. The same period also saw the birth (further south) of Vedāntadeśikāchāryya, the renowned Vaisnavite scholar and poet. There was also a similar Vaisnavite revival in Northern India due to the appearance of Rāmānanda and of his disciple Kabīr (1380–1420), whom both Hindus and Muhammadans equally honoured. Bengal under her Muhammadan rulers was also showing phenomenal literary and religious activity round Vaisnavism as its mainspring. She even won the heart of her alien ruler Nāsir Shah (1282–1325), who ordered the first Bengali rendering of the *Mahābhārata,* and is immortalized by the poet Vidyāpati through his dedication to him of one of his poems. It was about this time that Kīrttivāsa was translating the *Rāmāyaṇa* into Bengali and Māládhar Basu was employed by Husain Shāh to translate the *Bhāgavata Purāṇa.* The same period saw Vidyāpati Thākur singing the songs of Vaisnavism in Behar in the Maithili dialect; Chandidās singing in Bengal; and Mīrā Bāi in Mewar, until the spiritual soil and environment of the country were ripe for the birth of the two great religious leaders, each the founder of an independent sect of Vaisnavism, viz. Vallabha Āchāryya, who has still numerous followers in Central India, Bombay, and Gujarāt; and Śrī Chaitanya of Navadvīpa in Bengal (1485–1527), who was the cause of a profound intellectual and religious renaissance, the founder of a renovated Vaisnavism. He deluged the country with floods of spiritual enthusiasm that produced a bountiful crop of saints and singers and a vast and varied devotional literature. Thus the vitality of the national culture and civilization of the Hindus was still asserting itself while Tamerlane was harrying the political India under the Sultans of Delhi, and she was about to pass under Mogul monarchy. But Bengal was not merely active in poetry and religion, for Kullūka Bhatta was then writing his famous commentary on Manu and Jīmūtavāhana his great legal work *Dāyabhāga*, a task that was done for Behar and the West in the eleventh century by Vijñānesvara in his *Mitākṣarā*. It is indeed a remarkable fact that, under the adverse political conditions of the rule of the Sultans Hindu society evolved new means of self-protection against alien influence by means of rigorous domestic legislation as embodied in some of the most important *smṛiti* compilations which were all produced during this period. Thus Mādhavāchāryya, Viśveśvara Bhatta, Chandeśvara, Vāchaspati Misra, Āchāryya Chūḍāmaṇi, Pratāparudra, Raghunandana, and Kamalākara all flourished during this period and fixed Hindu social and domestic manners and customs in different parts of the country by their writings.

Under the Mogul Monarchy, as the literary historian of India so aptly remarks, 'Brahmanism remained with its undying vitality of intellectual life to continue its own course unmoved. The glorious reign of Akbar had seen an outbreak of native genius that, in its own lines, rivals that seen in England in Elizabethan times',[1] for, besides the many minor men of letters, there appeared in the Indian literary firmament the two shining stars, Sūrdās and Tulsidās, whose master pieces, according to Sir G. Grierson, are not far behind the work of Spenser and Shakespeare.

The phase of thought and religious emotion which uttered itself in the rapturous poetry of Jaya Deva received a continued expression through the great mystics of the Middle Ages, such as Vallabha, Mīrā Bāi, Bidyāpati, and the like, and the greater poets of Akbar's days, such as Kṛṣṇa Dās and the blind bard Sūrdās, while *Tulsi-krit-Rāmāyana* constitutes in itself the Vedas, Upanishads, and Purāṇas of the unlettered millions of Hindustān, to whom it presents their sole norm of conduct. In the reign of Jāhangīr the religion taught by Tulsidās was spread throughout Ajmere and Rajputana by the disciples of Dādu, a cotton cleaner of Ahmadabad, and founder of the Dādu Panthi sect.

Hindu India offers further evidence of her progress and capacity to bring forth great men. In 1469 was born Nānak, the founder of the religion of the Sikhs, and by the time of the fifth Guru, Arjuna (1581–1606), when the *Ādi Granth* formed the scriptures of the people, the Sikh faith had spread throughout the Jāt population of the Panjab and roused the fears

[1] Frazer's *Literary History of India*, p. 364.

of the Mogul monarchs. Arjuna was arrested and died from torture, but the event only fired his sect. Guru Har Govind (1606–38) roused the Sikh disciples to arms against the murderers of his father and sent them forth to blackmail the local governors of the Emperor Shāh Jahān. The ninth Guru, Teg Bahadur (1664–75) was cruelly tortured along with some Brahmans at Delhi, which only led to the national determination of the Sikhs to wage a religious war against Islam in India, to overthrow the Moslem political power and found a new empire on its ruins. The first step taken by the tenth Guru, Govind Singh, was to summon the aid of the Brahmans of Benares, propitiate the goddess Durgā, to whom six disciples offered themselves as sacrifices, and initiate himself and all his followers as members of the Khālsā or 'special property of the Guru'. Thus Sikhism and the Sikh power were most remarkable examples of the continued vitality and fertility of the motherland even under the depressing conditions of an alien domination.

Lastly, we have one more conspicuous example in the growth of the Marātha power for which the short-sighted bigotry of Aurangzebe was responsible. Indeed, it would appear that when the tyranny of Moslem rule was at its worst the life of Hindu India, far from being choked by the political powers, was asserting itself best and evolving out of its prolific vitality new means of meeting the oppression. Aurangzebe's cold contempt for Sivājī, 'the mountain rat', made it possible for that chief to weld the Marātha peasantry into a powerful soldiery whom a religious fanaticism and hatred of Islam developed into a power capable of exacting a tribute of one-fourth of all the revenue up to the limits of the English factory at Surat, away to the Marātha ditch dug round Calcutta as a defence against their raids. It is, however, to be borne in mind that this Hindu political power had, like most things Hindu, a religious origin and mission. The Guru of Sivājī was Rāmadās, the Brāhman, at whose feet he offered all his wealth and kingdom, which he consented to receive back only as a gift of his Guru, whose servant he always deemed himself; and accordingly the Marātha national flag was the red-ochre-coloured cloth worn by Sannyāsis. The other great spiritual leader of the movement was the Sudra poet, Tukārāma, whose asceticism and constant preaching and singing roused the slumbering spirit of the Marātha nation, and gave them a faith to live for and die for, the faith in Srīkṛṣna as the only way to salvation. As Frazer has justly remarked, 'The potential force of such a religious impulse is too often lost sight of by those who judge Indian life from a Western standpoint.'

The above broad and brief survey of the intellectual and spiritual progress and achievements of Hindu India, even under the adverse conditions of an aggressively alien rule, will, I hope, serve to establish the fact that these were ultimately due to a system of organization which had an independent existence and life of its own and was impenetrable to the foreign political powers who were unable to touch it for good or evil. The culture of the race was conserved and promoted through the indigenous machinery of appropriate institutions handed down from time immemorial, which embraced the manifold spheres of national life, economic and educational, social and religious. Thus the genius of the race was never in danger of being choked and stifled, for it was never in want of the adequate means of its self-expression. Thus also have Hindu culture and civilization been enabled to persist through the ages in spite of adverse political conditions, endowed with a singular capacity to survive the effects of alien rules and overcome the influence of political environment in general to which so many cultures and civilizations have succumbed in human history. Thus has Hindu India, justified in the peculiar institutions she has evolved, been enabled to successfully combat the otherwise irresistible influences of the state or political sovereignty, irrespective of the nationality or personnel of such sovereignty for the time being.

§ 2.

The subject of Local Self-Government in ancient India, besides its historical interest, is also possessed of an eminently practical interest. There are at present in India two contending schools of political thought proposing two different principles of administrative reform. One of these seeks to introduce self-government 'from above' and the other 'from below'. The truth perhaps lies in a duly combined application of both the principles, but, whatever may be the truth of the matter, it may, perhaps, be pertinent to point out that any form of provincial or central government which is organized merely 'from above', however mechanically perfect it may be, will fail to take a real root or gather to itself that vital force without which it will be a mere lifeless machine, a clog upon our national development, unless it is grafted in some way or other upon the spontaneous groupings of the people themselves as represented by their local self-governing institutions and based upon these natural foundations of *all* government. After all, it is the efficiency of the local institutions which matters most to the major part of the people, and, if self-government is the road to that efficiency, it should certainly be applied first to a sphere which directly touches the daily interests of popular life and its real welfare. It is, indeed, a mistaken judgement that seeks to associate self-government in India exclusively with that part of government which concerns India as a whole, for a people cannot be deemed to be essentially self-governing and enjoying the blessings of free institutions if they are without the right of themselves administering their local affairs and interests, on which their daily well-being depends. Besides, local government is itself the best school of political training for the masses living in the villages who cannot take part in the provincial or the central government except through their few representatives, and it is also to be cherished as a school of social service and a most efficient factor of social progress. Viewed in this light, the study of the ancient Indian local institutions will be interesting both to the government and to the people—to the *government*, because of their declared intention repeated in many resolutions and minutes to utilize and develop such remnants of indigenous local government as still exist in the country, and to shape the new upon the lines of the old;—to the *people*, because of their educative value. Such development will awaken a national self-respect and a reverence for institutions which, through the development of the appropriate social tissues, are fitted to successfully undertake the communal management of the school and the shrine, the relief of sickness and suffering, sanitation and poor relief, public works and public service, protection of life and property and settlement of disputes, and are thus able to preserve the integrity and independence of the culture of the race through the vicissitudes of its political fortunes.

The sphere of local government also exhibits a noteworthy democratic development in ancient India. A study of the institutions reflecting that development will throw considerable clear light not only on our early economic history, now shrouded in obscurity, but also on some of the basal factors of ancient Hindu culture and civilization. Respect for tradition and authority and a blind faith, rather than discriminating judgement, are generally supposed to be the primary formative factors of early Hindu society, despite the many manifestations of the democratic principle in such characteristically Hindu institutions as the joint family, the communal holding of land in the typical village community, and the like, as well as in the numerous self-governing, 'kingless' states in ancient India, the existence of which is attested by sober history.

It is too often forgotten that a great deal of socialism and communism (representing advanced democratic ideals of the modern age) is held in solution in the Indian social system. Appropriate expression is found through various institutions which all imply strong collectivistic or communistic sense and intuitions in the people, combined with a due restraint of that aggressive individualism and keen proprietary instinct which, under the influence of the Roman Jurisprudence, emphasizing private property and the sacredness of creditors' rights over those of the debtors', have given, in the opinion of the most thoughtful sociologists and political philosophers, a somewhat wrong direction to the development of nations and states in Europe.

§ 3.

It may perhaps be objected that the so-called democratic institutions, such as the village communities of ancient and mediaeval India, are merely survivals or continuations of tribal communism developing by mere aggregations and worked into compound forms. To make this objection is to mistake the fundamental tendencies reflected in the history of the evolution of tribal communities. That history shows that such communities may be either of the following types:

(*a*) As assemblies of elders, heads of families, &c., meeting on more or less equal terms to regulate common life.

(*b*) As constituted into central units under a single well-defined authority, generally an absolute head, such as the tribal head, patriarch, &c.

The first type is characteristic of the so-called Aryan peoples and follows a line of evolution which in Europe developed into the democratic city-states, with further differentiation of functions and the control of particularist tendencies by the development of central organs and by means of segregation, geographical as well as cultural; while in India the type culminated in the democratic institutions for the expression of corporate life, rural and urban.

The second type, characteristic of the so-called Semitic peoples, developed into great ancient monarchies of the East, such as the Egyptian, the Assyrian, and the Babylonian, by a mere re-duplication of similar parts. It may also be noted in this connexion that the Saracenic culture exhibits a crucial phenomenon in socio-political history, because there democracy has developed out of the absolutist institutions of the second type under the equalizing and levelling influences of Islamic religion.

Finally, it should also be understood that the Indian development of the local bodies really and fundamentally represents a distinctive type which must not be confounded with the rudiments of tribal self-government, invariably characteristic of primitive societies. The Indian institutions have developed differentiated structures and functions of their own, while the characteristic tendency of all tribal institutions (in the intermediate folk-stage) is to resolve into the original mass out of which they arise. Hence the councils of chieftains and elders in tribal communities, which are the repositories of tribal customs, derive their authority direct from the primary bodies which are represented *per capita* only and not by classes as in the Indian assemblies and unions.

We should therefore guard ourselves against these preliminary prejudices, objections, and misconceptions to which we are liable in studying the ancient local institutions of India by a reference to the history of tribal evolution and the fundamental distinction exhibited therein in the types of tribal culture-systems and institutions.

CHAPTER I

PRELIMINARY CONSIDERATIONS

THE sources of this study are twofold, viz. Literary and Epigraphic. In dealing with the literary evidence the following three possible orders suggest themselves, viz. (1) the order of chronology, (2) the order of organic development as traced in the historic course of origin and evolution, and (3) a logical order of ideal sequences and connexions. Inasmuch as the chronological order of early Indian culture-history has not yet been definitely fixed and ascertained, the first named has to be supplemented or modified by references to the other two orders. In the light of these considerations a method has been followed in the present inquiry which gathers together the available evidence on a particular topic and arranges it in the chronological order, seeking at the same time to trace the line of development and differentiation in successive stages.

There is another preliminary consideration which has to be observed in dealing with the evidence.

In treating the passages from literary works, and especially our law-books, as also those from the inscriptions, it is to be understood that the institutions to which they refer will be found to have exercised three classes of functions, viz. (*a*) industrial and commercial, (*b*) administrative, and (*c*) social or customary, including civic, educational, and religious. Each of these functions was exercised in accordance with definite rules and usages, some of them unwritten, others embodied in written agreements or charters as between the state and the assembly, or between the assembly and its members. The laws of associations, to which we shall refer later on, should therefore be understood to have a general scope and applicability, as comprehending the totality of these interests. A variety of terms has also to be used in correspondence with the variety of the institutions and of the functions they performed. Those terms, though necessarily general and almost abstract in their character, do not imply any looseness of social structure or function in relation to these institutions, but, on the contrary, indicate an organic inter-adaptation of social life and interests as well as a variety and flexibility characteristic of periods of exuberant growth.

Of the three broad classes of functions distinguished above with reference to the local institutions, we shall first deal with the industrial and commercial.

To the institutions representing these functions we shall apply the convenient term *guilds*, including trade-guilds, merchant-guilds, and craft-guilds, as the case may be, in view of the affinity in functions of these Indian institutions to their western counterparts.[1]

Before going into the evidence we are confronted by another difficulty, which it is best to discuss and deal with at the outset. We find that Sanskrit literature uses quite a number of terms with reference to these indigenous local bodies possessing various characters and functions. The communal life of ancient India, indeed, sought to express itself through a variety of institutions, civic and municipal, industrial and commercial, political and religious, and the evidence very often treats together all these diverse types of corporate life, thus making it difficult for the investigator to separate one from the other. There is, again, another difficulty to the inquirer, arising from a marked divergence of

[1] It is not, however, clear from our texts whether the same assembly exercised these various functions, or whether there were differently constituted and composed bodies for these different interests and works. There are, it will be seen, traces in the evidence furnished by the copper-plate inscriptions and grants, especially in southern India in the ninth and tenth centuries, of an elaborate and distinct machinery, popular in origin, though recognized and controlled by the state, having gradually appeared in the midst of the village communities themselves for the discharge of these various responsibilities of communal life.

opinion among the authoritative commentators as to the proper scope and meaning of the various terms employed in the original texts to indicate these popular local bodies. The following, for example, are the terms we generally come across in our literature, viz. *kula*, *gaṇa*. *jāti*, *pūga*, *vrāta*, *śreṇī*, *saṅgha*, *samudaya*, *samūha*, *sambhūya-samutthāna*, *pariṣat*, *charaṇa*. Most of these terms occur in the legal literature, which is characterized by the definiteness and precision of its phraseology and language, and yet the commentators very often differ in their interpretation of the same.

Thus, to take a few examples, the term *śreṇī* in Manu, VIII. 41,[1] is explained by Medhātithī[2] as 'guilds of merchants, artisans, bankers, Brahmans learned in the four Vedas', &c.; by Govindarāja, as 'guilds of merchants and *husbandmen*'; and by Nandana, as 'guilds of merchants and actors'.[3] The term *śreṇī* in Nārada I. 7[4] has been defined by one commentator as an assemblage of eminent *merchants* and by others as a company of *artisans*. The *Kauṭilīya* uses the word *śreṇī* in II. iv[5] in the sense

[1] जातिजानपदान्धर्मान् श्रेणीधर्मांश्च धर्मवित् । समीक्ष्यकुलधर्मांश्च स्वधर्मं प्रतिपालयेत् ॥

[2] एककार्यापन्नाः वणिक्कुरुकुसीद चातुर्विद्या दयः ।

[3] वणिक्कुशीलवादि ।

[4] कुलानि श्रेणयश्चैव गणाश्चाधिकृतोनृपः ।

[5] वास्तुच्छिद्रानुशालासेषु श्रेणीप्रवहणीनिकाया आवसेयुः ।

of guilds of workmen, but in VII. xvi[1] the word has a political reference, meaning a military clan; and in XI. i.[2] the term is applied to corporations that subsist by agriculture, trade, and military service, such as the Kāmbhojas, Surāṣṭras, and Kṣatriyas. The *Mahābhārata* uses the word in the sense of a guild of merchants [iii. 249. 16[3]; xii. 54. 20[4]]. Similarly, as regards the term *kula*, one commentator on Nārada, I. 7, takes it to mean an assemblage consisting of a few persons, and others as only a family meeting. The word in Yājñavalkya, II. 31[5] is explained by the *Mitākṣarā*[6] to mean an assemblage of kinsmen, relations, and friends. The same term is used in the *Kauṭilīya* [I. 17] in the sense of a council of regency or oligarchy, the rule of which is preferable to that of an incompetent king.[7] More various are the uses and interpretations of the term *gaṇa*,

[1] नित्यामित्रया श्रेणीबलं ।

[2] काम्भोजसुराष्ट्रक्षत्रियश्रेण्यादयो वार्त्ताशस्त्रोपजीविनः ।

[3] ब्राह्मणाः श्रेणिमुख्याश्च तथोदासीनवृत्तयः ।
किं मां वक्ष्यन्ति किंचापि प्रतिवक्ष्यामि तानहम् ॥

[4] शिष्टैश्च धर्मो यः प्रोक्तः स च मे हृदि वर्तते ।
देशजाति कुलानां च धर्मज्ञोऽस्मि जनार्दन ॥

[5] नृपेणाधिकृताः पूगाः श्रेणयोऽथ कुलानि च ।

[6] कुलानि ज्ञातिसम्बन्धिबन्धूनां समूहः ।

[7] न चैकपुत्रमविनीतं राज्ये स्थापयेत् ।

. . . . . .

कुलस्य वा भवेद्राज्यं कुलसङ्घो हि दुर्जयः ।
अराजव्यसनाबाधः शश्वदावसति क्षितिम् ॥

which in Manu, III. 164[1], is explained as meaning peoples or guilds. Govindarāja and Kullūka, commenting on the term in IV. 209,[2] mention as examples of such a fraternity of Brāhmaṇas inhabiting a monastery. The word in Nārada, I. 7, is explained by one commentator to mean a fellowship such as the Brāhmaṇa caste, and by others as an assembly of co-inhabitants, while the same word in X. 2[3] is explained, on the authority of Kātyāyana, to signify an assemblage of families. The *Mahābhārata* uses the term with reference to a political, self-governing corporation, which is also the sense of the word in such expressions as *Yaudheya gaṇasya*, occurring on the coins of the military clan of the Yaudheyas, and *Mālava-gaṇa-sthiti*, occurring in the Mandasor inscription of Kumāragupta. Nārada introduces in X. 2 a new term *Pūga*, which the *Vīramitrodaya* has interpreted in three senses, viz. (*a*) companies of traders and others, (*b*) associations of persons differing in caste whose mode of subsistence is not fixed, and (*c*) riders on elephants, horses, &c. Yājñavalkya [II. 31] has also used the term, and the *Mitākṣarā*[4] explains it as the assembly of the co-inhabitants of a village or town of different castes

[1] गणानां चैव याजकः।

[2] गणान्नं गणिकान्नं च विदुषा च जुगुप्सितम्।

[3] पाषण्डिनैगमश्रेणीपूगव्रातगणादिषु।

[4] पूगाः समूहाः भिन्नजातीनां भिन्नवृत्तीनां एकस्थाननिवासिनां यथा ग्रामनगरादयः।

and occupations, as distinguished from the *śreṇī*, which is the more limited assembly of persons belonging to a common craft or occupation, whether they be of the same or different castes. Some of these terms have been in use from times much earlier than those of our legal literature, since we find them used by Pāṇini, and the explanations by the *Kāśikā* are interesting. Pāṇini uses the terms *pūga*, *gaṇa*, and *saṅgha* in V. 2. 52,[1] *pūga* in V. 3. 112,[2] *vrāta* in V. 3 113,[3] and *saṅgha* in V. 3. 114.[4] The *Kāśikā* uses *saṅgha* in the generic sense to mean the larger assembly or corporation, of which the *pūga*, *vrāta*, &c. are varieties. Thus, the *pūga* is a special kind of *saṅgha*, an association of men of various castes who, having no fixed occupation or means of livelihood, unite in the pursuit of wealth and pleasure as their main aim[5]; the *vrāta* again is an association of men of different castes having no definite means of subsistance, and living by bodily labour or violence,[6] like the *Kāpotapākyaḥ* or wild community making its living by pigeon-hunting, &c. Pāṇini also uses the word *śreṇī* in II. 1. 59,[7] which has been ex-

1 बहुपूगगणसंघस्य तिथुक् ।

2 पूगाञ्ञ्योऽग्रामणीपूर्वात् ।

3 व्रातच्फञोरस्त्रियाम् ।

4 आयुधजीविसंघाञ्ञ्यड्वाहीकेष्वब्राह्मणराजन्यात् ।

5 नानाजातीयाः अनियतवृत्तयः अर्थकामप्रधानाः संघाः पूगाः ।

6 नानाजातीयाः अनियतवृत्तयः उत्सेधजीविनः संघाः व्राताः ।

7 श्रेण्यादयः कृतादिभिः ।

plained by both *Kayyata* and *Tattvabodhinī* as an assembly of persons following a common craft or trading in a common commodity.[1] Lastly, Pāṇini mentions certain corporations or *saṅghas* that live by the profession of arms, e. g. the *Mallāḥ*, the *Yaudheyas*, &c., of which class the *Kāśikā* names more than seventy examples.[2] The *Kauṭilīya* confines the sense of the term *saṅgha* to that of a political corporation [XI. i].[3]

On a closer and critical consideration of these various terms, their usages and interpretations, it

[1] एकेन शिल्पेन पण्येन वा ये जीवन्ति तेषां समूहः श्रेणिः ।

[2] The *Kāśikā* mentions as examples of *pūgas* (1) *Lauhadhvajyah*, i. e. those that have as their emblem something that is made of copper, the red metal; the *Tattvabodhinī* reads *lauhitadhvajyah*, to signify a body of persons having a red flag as their emblem; (2) *Saibya*, perhaps the 'Siboi', the wild tribe with a republican constitution subdued by Alexander; (3) *Chātakya*; (4) *Devadattaka*, the tribe led by Devadatta; as examples of *vrāta*, besides (1) *Kapotapākyah*, we have (2) *Vraihimatyah*, a non-Brahmanical people (*St. Petersburg Dict.*); (3) *Kannjāyanyah*, perhaps the kingless tribe of *Ārjunāyanas* [see V. A. Smith's *Early History of India*, third ed., p. 286]; and (4) *Brādhuāyanya*.

[3] संघवृत्तम् । In the Jaina literature, e. g. *Kalpasūtra*, the terms *gaṇa*, *kula*, and *śākhā* are used in distinct senses. *Gaṇa* designates the school derived from one teacher; *kula*, the succession of teachers in one line; *śākhā*, the lines which branch off from one teacher. The Jaina inscriptions of Mathurā assigned to the age of Kaniṣka [*Ep. Ind.*, vols. I and II] constantly use the terms *gaṇa*, *kula*, *śākhā*, and sometimes *sambhoga* [Lüders's List, no. 27], e. g. the *Kottiya* (*Kauṭṭika*) *gaṇa*, the *Ṭhāniya* (*sthānīya*) *kula*, the *Śrīgṛiha sambhoga*, the *Āryyaverī* (*ārya-vajrī*) *śākhā*. In the *Vinaya*, vol. IV, p. 226, there is mention of *saṅgha*, *gaṇa*, *pūga*, and *seṇī*. The terms occur in other places too.

will be found that the variety is not without underlying unity, and that the complexity of annotations is reducible to a comprehensible simplicity. Thus, the majority of the authorities, e.g. Manu, Nārada, Kauṭilya, the *Mahābhārata*, and the like, agree in having employed the term *śreṇī* to mean *guild*, whether it be the guild of artisans, agriculturists, or merchants, i. e. the craft-guild, trade- or merchant-guild; while a similar sense has been fixed for the term *Pūga* by authorities like the *Kaśikā*, the *Mitākṣarā*, and the *Vīramitrodaya*. The other two terms, *saṅgha* and *gaṇa*, apparently were used by the earlier authorities like Pāṇini, Kauṭilya, and the *Mahābhārata* in a political signification to mean autonomous, *kingless* clans or corporations as distinguished from *kingships*.

The existence of these various terms is in itself a strong evidence demonstrating the reality of the institutions designated. We shall now go into the details of that evidence scattered throughout our literature, and shall try to piece them together so as to trace the continuity of the life and history of these ancient local institutions and unfold the process of their evolution through the ages. As has been already stated, we shall first of all deal with the development of self-government in the sphere of industrial and commercial interests, and shall accordingly trace the history and evolution of what may be called the ancient Hindu guilds.

CHAPTER II

THE POSITION OF THE GUILD IN LITERATURE

According to orthodox Hindu tradition and opinion, the origins of Hindu culture and civilization in all respects and particulars, aspects and phases, strata and stages, are to be found foreshadowed and imbedded in the Vedas. To these eternal and original documents can be traced the roots of all our subsequent history and development. Whatever may be the intrinsic worth and merits of this theory, it seems to be true at least in respect of the history of Hindu guilds. Even foreign scholars such as Geldner, Roth, &c., for instance, find references to them in the Vedic literature. There is no doubt a difference of opinion among Vedic scholars as to the exact significance of these references, and, considered by themselves merely as literary passages, they may seem to be doubtful indications of a formal and well-defined institution. But if we relate to the *literary* evidence the evidence of *history*, the evidence furnished by the evolution of Aryan life, the spread of Aryan colonization, the propagation of Aryan culture and civilization in India from the Vedic period downwards, much of the uncertainty of the purely literary evidence will disappear. The fact of the matter is that Vedic society was sufficiently settled to admit of an elaborate differentiation of functions and occupations among the people, and already presented an economic environment favourable to the growth of industrial and commercial combinations in the community, leading to the formation of specialized institutions like the guilds. These were perhaps natural and necessary growths out of the conditions and requirements of the economic life of the age with its many-sided development. It is admitted on all hands that Vedic society at a comparatively early period divided itself into three fundamental orders, estates, or castes, viz.: (1) the ruling caste or the warrior-caste, comprising the king and his *entourage*, his great lords and vassals, the knights of the army; (2) the priestly caste, distinguished in learning and religion, which, though not directly wielding any political or martial power, was possessed of supreme influence in the state as regulating the king's will—an influence which rested solely on its high character and spirituality; (3) the people-caste with its Aryan blood and eligibility for all Aryan privileges in the matter of legal rights, religious rites, and educational opportunities. These three were the twice-born classes, but to them was added a fourth, the un-Aryan, merely 'once-born', deprived of good birth, devoid of spiritual or legal privileges, of the rights of property, comprising the remnant of a displaced native population, the degraded branches or illegitimate descendants of the pure castes, and also foreigners, so as to constitute a mixed class of out-castes, pursuing means of livelihood not sanctioned for the pure. All these castes or classes were, from the political point of view, well-organized units with defined status and occupations, except the people-caste where we have an internal classification in three well-organized bodies, socially and economically apart from one another. Historically, these three sub-castes were (1) the great body of ranchmen, the cattle-raising population, with their dependants, the herdsmen and cow-boys; (2) the agriculturists or farmers who raised grain, and their supplementary associates who raised fruit and vegetables; and (3) the entire trading population, whether by land or by sea, maintaining active intercourse with foreign merchants. As Kauṭilya[1] puts it, the three legitimate occupations which the Vaiśya should follow to earn a living are Kṛṣi, Pāśupālya, and Vānijya, i. e. Agriculture, Cattle-raising, and Trade. Subsidiary occupations developed in connexion with these,

[1] वैश्यस्याध्ययनं यजनं दानं कृषिपाशुपाल्ये वणिज्या च। [I. iii.]

such as money-lending which, despised at first, became afterwards a recognized occupation for the twice-born. There were also the mechanics, artisans, carpenters, peddlers and the like, and the line between legitimate and objectionable labour was very often crossed, as is proved by the frequent denunciations in our legal literature of those that did so, and also by the relaxation of the legal strictness in cases of distress due to failure of legitimate living.[1] There were thus in course of development three specialized sub-castes dividing the unity of the people-caste, each pursuing its particular interests to the exclusion of other interests, so that ultimately the traders as a class made themselves into a distinct body, apart from the classes to whom belonged the care of agriculture and cattle. Thus the due development of the commercial interests of the country was secured, leading to the establishment of guilds. The same thing happened also in the case of the artisan class or the Sūdras, who were, of course, legitimate members of the Aryan body-politic with their occupations defined. These were, in the words of Kauṭilya (a very early authority), 'Vārta, Kāru, Kuśilava, Karma cha', i. e. agriculture, cattle-rearing, and trade, together with manufactures

[1] *Gautama*, VII. 6 and VII. 25; *Vasiṣṭha*, II. 22 and III. 24; *Manu*, VIII. 348 and X. 81; *Baudhāyana*, II. 4, 16, II. 2, 4, 18; *Viṣṇu*, II. 15.

and practice of such arts as acting and the like, thus showing that the line of demarcation separating the occupations of the Vaiśya from those of the lower caste was not very rigid.[1]

We thus see that guilds were but natural and necessary growths at a very early period of our history, due to the considerable progress which the country had achieved in arts, manufactures, and trade. They presuppose and imply in fact a development to which history testifies. And so when we consider the story of that development, the facts in the commercial and industrial life of Vedic India which can be gathered from the numerous references to trade and manufactures with which Vedic literature is replete—references which it is not the purpose of this monograph to bring together—we should not be surprised by the references to the guilds which some scholars find in the Vedas. The fact of the matter is that guilds or commercial associations must always wait on a certain degree of development to be attained by the particular com-

[1] The above account is on the lines of the lucid exposition of Hopkins in the *JAOS.*, vol. XIII, pp. 72–81. I have not entered here into the vexed question, which is irrelevant to my present purpose, of the origin and development of these social classes and industrial groups, or how far they were rigidly differentiated from one another in functions and their spheres of interests. It is to be understood that the Vedic period comprises not merely that of the Saṃhitās, but also that of the Brāhmaṇas and Upaniṣads. The early Sūtra literature is not included.

mercial or industrial interests concerned; guild-life in fact belongs to a considerably advanced stage of economic progress in which the individual mechanics, artisans, or traders have sufficient business instincts developed in them, and have achieved sufficient success in their several businesses to appreciate the necessity of organizing themselves into a community for the purpose of promoting their individual and collective interests. The growth of guilds thus means that the industrial units are sufficiently efficient to partake of a public life and regulate themselves by common rules as parts of a whole or a common organism. The extent to which the differentiation of economic functions or occupations was carried even in the Vedic period of our history will seem to point to the conclusion that those scholars who choose to find in certain passages from Vedic literature proofs of the existence of guilds cannot very well be considered as being guilty of making an extravagant claim and taking up an untenable position. The existence of such institutions is not quite out of relation to the economic progress of the period with its evolution and differentiation of numerous arts and crafts and of occupational castes jealously safeguarding their several interests as explained above.

Let us now proceed to the Vedic passages themselves. All of these contain the use of the words *śreṣṭhin* and *śraiṣṭhya*, which from their contexts would appear to have respectively the sense of the 'headman of a guild' and 'the foremost place that belongs to such a headman, the presidency of a guild'.[1]

Thus the *Aitareya Brāhmaṇa* has three passages bearing on the subject. In III. 30. 3[2] there is a reference to the position of the chief of the guild (*śreṣṭhi*) who favours with a draught from his goblet

[1] '*Śreṣṭhin* occurs in several passages of the Brāhmaṇas where the St. Petersburg Dictionary assigns to the word the sense of "a man of consequence". It is, however, possible that the word may already have had the sense of the headman of a guild, the modern Seth. There is a similar doubt in the use of *śraiṣṭhya*, which is perhaps not merely "the foremost place" as usually assumed, but definitely "the presidency of a guild"'.—Macdonell and Keith, *Vedic Index*, vol. II, pp. 403–4.

[2] श्रेष्ठी पात्रे रोचयत्येव यं कामयतेतम् ।

Sāyaṇa explains the passage thus:

> 'For that very reason (in this world) also a merchant prince, desirous of rendering acceptable a dependant of his to others refusing to own him, has nevertheless the power to enforce the grant to him of a worthy position by them, in spite of his disqualification due to violation of social rules.'

(श्रेष्ठी कश्चित् धनपतिः यं स्वकी यं भृत्यं इतरैः अनङ्गीकृतमपि सर्वेभ्यो रोचयितुं कामयते तं भृत्यं आचारहीनं पात्रे प्रतिग्रहयोग्य-स्थाने बलात् सर्वेभ्यो रोचयत्येव)

Martin Haug translates the passages thus:

> 'Thus it comes that a chief favours with a draught from his goblet whom he likes.'

Both these interpretations agree in ascribing to the chief much social power and influence, and the chief is considered by noted Vedic scholars to be the chief of a guild.

whom he likes. In IV. 25. 8–9 and again in VII. 18. 8[1] the position of leadership is indicated by the use of the words *śraiṣṭhya* and *śreṣṭhatā*. In the *Śatapatha Brāhmaṇa* XIII. 7. 1. 1[2] the word *śraiṣṭhya* is similarly used to indicate lordship. In the *Atharva Veda* I. 9. 3[3] there is the expression 'bestow on him lordship (*śraiṣṭhya*) over his fellows' and in X. 6. 31[4] the word *śraiṣṭhya* is again used in that sense. The terms *śreṣṭhin* and *śraiṣṭhya* are similarly used to denote the chief of the guild or the high position that belong to him among his fellows in the *Chāndogya Upaniṣad*, V. 2. 6[5]; *Kauṣitaki Upaniṣad*, IV. 20, II. 6, and IV. 15. 20. In all these references from the Vedic literature the manner of the allusion to the head of the guild, and his high social position and pre-eminent influence seems to support the conclusion expressed by some Vedic scholars that the guild was then already a known and familiar institution, a commonplace phenomenon, an ordinary object of daily observation, to which, as to matters of every day experience, references are made in order to explain abstruse and abstract philosophical subjects, topics,

[1] धृत्यै श्रैष्ठ्याय गाधिनाः ।
[2] सर्वेषां भूतानां श्रैष्ठ्यं ।
[3] सजातानां श्रैष्ठ्य आ धेह्येनम् ।
[4] मणिः श्रैष्ठ्याय मूर्धतः ।
[5] श्रैष्ठ्यᳫ राज्य माधिपत्यं ।

or problems. Metaphorical and indirect allusions to guilds show that they are already well-known existences within the range of common observation, and the allusions are warranted on the logical principle of arguing from the known to the unknown, of explaining the unknown, the unfamiliar and the abstract in the terms of the known, the familiar, and the concrete.

What tends to lend additional force to the aforesaid suggestion is that these Vedic passages are not solitary in the particular significance read into them. The same tradition is repeated, and, that in no uncertain terms, by the two Epics and even by some of the Pāli works. In the procession of citizens who accompanied Bharata in his quest of Rāma figured the gem-cutters, potters, weavers, armourers, ivory-workers, 'well-known goldsmiths', the foremost merchants and citizens of all classes, so that the *Rāmāyaṇa* recognizes the importance of the position held by the trades and crafts in society.[1] The *Mahāvaṃsa* also in the same way represents the heads of the five trades as being the chosen messengers entrusted with the dignified duty of carrying a welcome from Kitti Sirimegha to his son Parākrama, afterwards Parākrama Bāhu the Great. In Bāna's *Harṣa Charita* we are told that in con-

[1] II. 83. 12, 13: ये च तत्रापरेसर्वे सम्मता ये च नैगमाः । &c.

nexion with the preparations for the marriage of a princess were summoned from every country 'companies of skilled artists'. Similarly in the preparations described in the *Harivaṃsa* for the witnessing of the contest between Kṛṣṇa and Balarāma by the royal family and citizens of Mathurā, we are told of the pavilions of the different companies and corporations with banners representing the implements and emblems of the several crafts.[1] The *Mahābhārata* mentions a prince who, defeated in battle and ashamed to return home, exclaims: 'For what shall I have to say to my relatives, to the priests and to the heads of the guilds (गण्यमुख्याः) ?' [III. 249. 16]. But besides the social importance of the guilds and their chiefs the *Mahābhārata* sets forth their political importance to the state. Their power is to be appreciated by the king as much as that of his mercenary army. Their heads must be 'talked over' by spies when the king projects the conquest of another kingdom. Their strength lies in union and their weakness in dissension. The king is especially charged not to tax them too heavily lest they become disaffected, and their disaffection is represented as a calamity. They may be controlled by the king by bribery and by fomenting discord. [See XII. 107 which deals with the *gaṇas* in detail.]

[1] स्वकर्म द्रव्ययुक्ताभिः पताकाभिर्निरन्तरम् ।
श्रेणीनां च गणानां च मञ्चा भान्त्यचलोपमाः ॥

The high social position of the *śreṣṭhin* as hinted at in the Vedic passages is very well brought out in some of the Pāli works. While Sanskrit literature mentions guilds of various characters, the Buddhist literature seems to bring into prominence one class of guilds in particular, viz. ths merchant guilds. In the story of the Buddha's life an important period of the life is intimately associated with the great Śeṭh families of Benares and some neighbouring towns whose recognized social position and influence, when enlisted on behalf of the new faith contributed materially to its popularity and propagation in the early and critical stage of its career. Thus the *Chullavagga* [V. 8 and VI. 1. 4] mentions the *seṭṭhi* of Rājagaha; the *Mahāvagga* [I. 7. 1] mentions Yasa, the son of a *seṭṭhi* of Benares and [VIII. 1. 16, &c.] the *seṭṭhi* of Rājagaha. The *Mahāvaṁsa* mentions an office called *seṭṭhitā* to which the king was to appoint. *Jātaka*, I. 120–122, mentions an office of *seṭṭhi* (*seṭṭhi-tthāna*) in a city, which was conferred only on such as possessed the requisite wealth and talent. Anātha Piṇḍika, the merchant prince famous for his gift to the Buddha of the Jetavana park, is mentioned as the *seṭṭhi* standing alone or as the *Mahā-seṭṭhi* in *Jāt.* I. 95. 231–232. The position of the foreman of the guild is also indicated in *Jāt.* II. 12. 52[1] and III. 281[2] where he

[1] 'Senipamukhā.'

[2] 'The principal smith of the thousand (*Jeṭṭhaka*).'

is an important minister in attendance upon the king. In *Jāt.* IV. 43[1] there is a reference to an office of judgeship of all the merchant guilds—an office which did not exist before, and to that office was appointed the king's treasurer. The heads of guilds (*seṇiyo*) are called *pamukha* (president) and also *jeṭṭhaka* (elder, alderman), the distinction between the two terms not being apparent. *Jāt.* II. 18 mentions the division in one of the large centres of wood-craft of the population of 1,000 families into two equal groups each under one *Jeṭṭhaka.* Similarly the groups of mariners [*Jāt.* IV. 137],[2] garland-makers [*Jāt.* III. 405],[3] caravan-traders [*Jāt.* I. 368[4]; II. 295],[5] the moss-troopers numbering 500 of a 'little robber village' in the hills, e.g. near Uttarapañchāla [*Jāt.* I. 296. 297[6]; II. 388[7]; IV. 430.[8] 433 Com.] and the

[1] 'Then the king gave him the post of Treasurer, and with it went the judgeship of all the merchant guilds. Before that no such office existed.' [*Sabbaseṇīnaṁ vichāraṇārahaṁ bhaṇḍāgārikaṭṭhānaṁ.*]

[2] 'Niyyāmakajeṭṭhako.'

[3] 'Mālakārajeṭṭhakassa.'

[4] 'Once upon a time when Brahmadatta was reigning in Benares the Bodhisatta came to life as the leader of a caravan.'

[5] 'Satthavāhajeṭṭhako' (merchant-leader, caravan-chief).

[6] 'Now the border was harried by robbers from the mountains; and they made a raid one day on the village where the pair lived . . . the girl was taken to wife by the robber chieftain.'

[7] 'He gathered 500 robbers and became their chief, and lived by highway robbery.'

[8] 'Up wind from this hill was a robber village where 500 robbers dwelt.'

forest police who escorted travellers [*Jāt.* II. 335 [1]] were all organized under a *Jeṭṭhaka*. Then there were the trade-guilds [*Jāt.* IV. 411], eighteen in number, whom the king summons to witness his procedure or to accompany him [*Jāt.* VI. 22],[2] of which are specifically mentioned as 'masons, blacksmiths, carpenters, painters, men skilled in all arts and crafts' [*Jāt.* VI. 427 [3]; *Mil. Panh.* I. 2].[4] Similarly the 'elder' of a village of 1,000 smiths in whom were combined the functions of the head man of the village, the village syndic, and president of the local guild, is described as 'a favourite of the king (of Benares) rich and of great substance' [*Jāt.* III. no. 387].

It is thus clear from the above references that the merchant (*seṭṭhi*) attained at a very early time to a position of much social importance. This was

1 '... the Bodhisatta born ... a forester took the lead of a band of 500 foresters .... He used to hire himself out to guide men through it ... a merchant's son arrived with a caravan of 500 wagons ... offered him 1,000 pieces to be his guide through the forest ... in the midst of the forest up rose 500 robbers ... the head forester alone put to flight all the 500 robbers.'

2 'The king ... assembled the four castes, the eighteen guilds' ...

3 'The Great Being ... took with him eighteen companies of men, masons, blacksmiths, carpenters, painters, men skilled in all arts and crafts.'

4 'Guilds of traders in all sorts of finery display their goods in the bazaars that face all quarters of the sky', in the city of Sāgala, 'a great centre of trade', 'in the country of the Yonakas.' There is an interesting enumeration of various crafts and trades in *Mil. Panh.* V. 4.

chiefly due to his possession of great wealth derived from trade. Many of these merchants were like millionaires of modern times; we read of a merchant's son as leading a caravan of 500 wagons. They seem to have been the principal representatives of the householder (*gahapati*) class, the typical burghers of the great towns. Besides being private traders they are also mentioned as representatives of commerce holding an official position in the court. It may perhaps be very reasonably assumed that the association of these merchant-princes with the Buddha acted as an effective adventitious aid in advertising the solitary and self-absorbed ascetic, until even the attentions of crowned heads and emperors, like Bimbisār and Ajātasatru of the Magadhan throne, were drawn to that divine beggar. It was again their munificent financial support and endowment of Buddhism in its very early stages that probably paved the way for its popularity and propagation among the masses. The Buddha's conversion of the upper classes of society easily established his influence and made it felt among the lower classes or the masses.[1]

[1] It is this 'marked leaning to aristocracy in ancient Buddhism' which has led Hermann Oldenberg to remark that 'it seems as if the actual composition of the band which surrounded Buddha's person, and the composition of the early church especially was by no means in due keeping with the theory of equality' professed by Buddhism, which did not reserve to Brahmans only the right of

entry into a spiritual life, but acknowledged the equal right of all persons without distinction to be received into the order. The Buddha himself describes the actual situation when in his first sermon at Benares he speaks of the supreme religious enlightenment for the sake of which 'the sons of noble families (*kulaputtā*) leave their homes and go into homelessness', for here were 'young *Brahmans* like Sāriputta, Moggallāna, Kaccāna, *nobles* like Ānanda, Rāhula, Anuruddha, sons of the greatest *merchants* and highest municipal dignitaries, like Yasa, invariably men and youths of the most respectable classes of society, and with an education in keeping with their social status'. 'Prominent among the "adherents" stand also the two *royal friends* of Buddha, Bimbisāra, the ruler of Magadha, and Pasenadi, the ruler of Kosala, both approximately of the same age as Buddha, and throughout their lives true protectors of his church. Then comes Jīvaka, the renowned physician-in-ordinary to Bimbisāra, who was appointed by the king to undertake medical attendance, not on him and his women only, but also on Buddha and Buddha's order; next, the merchant Anāthapindika, who had presented to the order the garden of Jetavana, Buddha's favourite place of resort. In all important places which Buddha touched in the course of his wanderings he found bands of such lay-believers, who went out to meet him, arranged for assemblies in which Buddha spoke, who gave him and his companions their meals, who placed their residences and gardens at their disposal, or made them over to the order as church property. If he went wandering about with hundreds of his disciples, pious votaries were sure to accompany him on his journey with carts and waggons, and they brought necessaries of life, salt, and oil with them, for each in his turn to prepare the wanderer a meal, and crowds of needy folk followed in their train to snatch the remains of these provisions.' And not alone were *male* adherents in the circle of Buddha's followers. For we find the *women* of India zealously engaged as fellow-labourers through charity, assistance, and service, in those practical spheres which the young church opened up for religious usefulness. *The stupendous munificence which met the Buddhist order at every step proceeded in great measure, perhaps in the greatest measure, from women* of whom the typical representative was the honourable matron *Viśākhā*, a rich citizen commoner at

Sāvatthi, who made the first liberal preparations on a large scale to provide for Buddha's disciples who came to Sāvatthi the chief necessaries of life. For this she thus spoke to Buddha to obtain this permission: 'I desire as long as I live, sire, to give the brotherhood clothes for the rainy season, to give food to stranger monks who arrive here, to give food to monks who are passing through, to give food to sick brethren, to give food to the attendants on the sick, to give medicine to the sick, to distribute a daily dole of cooked rice, to give bathing-dresses to the sisterhood of nuns.' Pictures like this of Viśākhā, benefactresses of the church, with their inexhaustible religious zeal, and their not less inexhaustible resources of money, are certainly, if anything ever was, drawn from the life of India in those days: they cannot be left out of sight, if we desire to get an idea of the actors who made the oldest Buddhist community what it was. [Oldenberg, *Buddha*, pp. 155–69.]

CHAPTER III

§ I

ORGANIZATION OF GUILDS

We shall now deal with the evidence regarding the organization of the guilds, their scope, functions, and laws.

The efficiency of the organization will be apparent from the laws relating to apprenticeship. These are thus stated by Nārada:

'If (a young man) wishes to be initiated into the art of his own craft, with the sanction of his relations, he must go and live with a master,[1] the duration of his apprenticeship having been fixed.

The master shall teach him at his own house and feed him. He must not employ him in work of a different description, and should treat him like a son.

If one forsakes a master, who instructs him and

[1] Cf. *Bṛhaspati*, XVI. 6: 'Arts (consisting of) work in gold, base metals and the like, and the art of dancing and the rest, are termed human knowledge; he who studies them should do work at his teacher's house.'

whose character is unexceptionable, he may be compelled by forcible means to remain (at the master's house), and he deserves corporal punishment[1] and confinement.

Though his course of instruction be completed, an apprentice must continue to reside at the house of his master till the fixed period has expired. The profit of whatever work he may be doing there belongs to his master.

When he has learnt the art of his craft within the (stipulated) period, the apprentice shall reward his master as plentifully as he can, and return home, after having taken leave of him.

Or, a certain fee having been agreed upon and the skill of the pupil examined, the apprentice shall take (his fee) and shall not go to live in the house of another man.'[2]

[1] Similarly Manu, IV. 16J; VII. 268–300: *Gautama*, II. 43–4; *Āpastamba*, I. 8. 30; *Viṣñu*, LXXXI. 81–2.

[2] स्वशिल्पमिच्छन्नाहर्तुं बान्धवानामनुज्ञया ।
आचार्यस्य वसेदन्ते कालं कृत्वा सुनिश्चितम् ॥
आचार्यः शिक्षयेदेनं स्वगृहे दत्तभोजनम् ।
नचान्यत्कारयेत्कर्म पुत्रवच्चैनमाचरेत् ॥
शिक्षयन्तमदुष्टं च य आचार्यं संपरित्यजेत् ।
बलाद्वासयितव्यः स्याद्वधबन्धौ च सोऽर्हति ॥
शिक्षितोऽपि कृतं कालमन्तेवासीसमाप्नुयात् ।
तत्र कर्म च यत्कुर्यादाचार्यस्यैव तत्फलम् ॥
गृहीतशिल्पः समये कृत्वाचार्यप्रदक्षिणाम् ।
शक्तितश्चानुमान्यैनमन्तेवासी निवर्तते ॥

The above rules bring out several important and interesting features. In the first place, there was the system of indenture under which the apprentice and the master were bound to each other for a fixed period stated in the deed. As Vīramitrodaya points out, the teacher must make an agreement in this form, 'Let this apprentice stay with me so and so long'. In the second place, the indenture emphasizes equally and fairly the obligations of both the master and the apprentice. As regards the obligations of the master, he had to adopt the apprentice as his own son, and treat and feed him as such. He should teach him whole-heartedly and honestly; the master was competent to make him do the work strictly related to the craft he was learning but was not competent to exploit his labour or skill by employing it for purposes unconnected with it. While making

वेतनं वा यदि कृतं ज्ञात्वाशिष्यस्य कौशलम् ।
अन्तेवासी समादद्यान्न चान्यस्य गृहे वसेत् ॥

[V. 16–21.]

The translation is that of Jolly in the *S. B. E.*, vol. XXXIII. In V. 18 the word *aduṣṭam* may be taken as an adverb modifying the verb *śikṣyantam*, in which case the translation will be: 'If one forsakes a teacher who instructs him properly,' &c. In V. 20 Jolly seems to take the word *pradakṣiṇām* as a gift, but it usually means circumambulation, which the apprentice is to perform as a mark of respect for the master. The meaning of V. 21, which is rather vague in Jolly's translation, seems to be: 'If, however, a salary be fixed befitting his skill, the pupil should accept it, and should not go to stay (i. e. accept appointment) in the house of another (craftsman).'

him work thus, he should not treat the apprentice like a hired labourer but like a son, with due tenderness and affection. Equally strict were the obligations under which the apprentice was bound to his master. If through the master's efficient training he attains proficiency in the craft before the expiry of the period stipulated for in the indenture, he was not competent to leave the master but had to serve out his full term, cheerfully yielding to him the fruits of his labour as the reward or compensation for the saving of time effected by the superior skill of the master in teaching. Yājñavalkya [II. 187][1] states the same condition thus: 'Even if one has learnt the art (within the prescribed time) he must live in the house of one's teacher for the full period of contract. The student, desirous of learning an art, who has received his board from the teacher, must make over to the latter the fruits of his labour (during the period of his pupilage). Thus Yājñavalkya justifies the master's appropriation of the results of all work done by his pupil during his apprenticeship as a sort of compensation for the expenses he incurs in giving him free board, lodging, and tuition. The master was also empowered to compel the return of a runaway apprentice, whom

[1] कृतशिल्पोऽपि निवसेत् कृतकालं गुरोर्गृहे ।
अन्तेवासी गुरुप्राप्तभोजनस्तत्फलप्रदः ॥

he could flog or confine for his disobedience, provided such disobedience or desertion was not by way of protest against any mortal sin or other heavy crime committed by the master. This is no doubt a characteristically Hindu provision securing the moral purity of craftsmen to which modern industrial legislation is hardly sufficiently attentive. There is again another provision for the payment of a salary to the pupil adequate to his proficiency if it was desired by the master to retain his services, in which case the first claim upon his services belongs to his master.

Lastly, the pupil is recommended to be always humble before his master in the following quaint exhortation: 'For science is like a river, ever advancing to a humbler level; therefore as one's knowledge grows broader and deeper one should become ever more humble towards the source of of one's knowledge' [V. 12].

This exhortation is indeed symbolical and characteristic of the sacred and spiritual relations[1] that normally obtained between the master-craftsman

[1] Cf. *Mahāvagga*, I. 32. 1: 'The *achariya*, O Bhikkhus, ought to consider the *antevāsika* as a son; the *antevāsika* ought to consider the *achariya* as a father. Thus these two, united by mutual reverence, confidence, and communion of life, will progress, advance, and reach a high stage in this doctrine and discipline.

I prescribe, O Bhikkhus, that you live (the first) ten years in dependence on an *achariya* . . .'

and his apprentices—relations which were the direct outcome of the peculiar educational system and environment under which they worked. To these wholesome relations, and especially to the superior educational efficacy of the system which produced them, is to be traced the signal success which is admitted on all hands to have been achieved by the handicraftsmen of ancient and mediaeval India, and which so largely enabled her to command for much more than a thousand years (from Pliny to Tavernier) the markets of the East as well as the West, and secured to her an easy and universally recognized pre-eminence among the nations of the world in exports and manufactures. We are, however, more concerned with the system than its success, with the methods of training than their results, the character of the educational machinery and organization than the record of its magnificent outputs. The essence of the whole scheme or system, the fundamental feature on which it rests, is that the young craftsman is brought up and educated in the actual workshop of his master whose disciple he is, although the master may sometimes be even his father. This means that the pupil stands in a peculiar relation to his master, a sacred relation of devoted personal service and attachment in which alone can the learner best imbibe and most naturally and spontaneously assimilate the special excellences of his teacher, his true inward method, nay, even his trade secrets which can no longer be hidden from one whom he has adopted as his son. The very intimacy and depth of the personal relationship between the teacher and the taught solves substantially the difficulties of the educative process, which is impossible in the case of the busy professor at a modern technical school where he is concerned with his students for a few hours in the week, and has no opportunity of associating them with his main business in which he is called upon to show his real worth and exercise his best talent. And this brings us to the other aspect of our indigenous organization, viz., training in the actual workshop where the teaching is learnt from the very beginning and in relation to real things, difficulties, and problems, and primarily by service, by personal attendance on the master. And it is not only technique that is learnt but something more valuable: in the workshop there is life itself, besides mere plant and tools, for the workshop is part of a home, which relieves its mechanical monotony and places the pupil in touch with life and its difficulties, human relationships, culture, and religion, whereby his heart is trained as much as his hand—a thing which is as necessary to art as mere technique.

There is one other noticeable feature in connexion with the rules of apprenticeship as explained by Nārada. It is that the considerations of caste did not affect the admission of apprentices into a craft. The only consideration that mattered was the consent of the apprentice's guardian and relations, and when that was obtained the youth was free to learn the craft which he affected. This shows that the barriers between occupations were not so fixed and rigid as those between castes. This is proved not only by the aforesaid solitary rule stated by Nārada, but by the universal permissive regulation contained in all the important law-books, authorizing the twice-born classes to take to an occupation of an inferior caste, in times of distress or failure, to obtain a living through lawful labour.[1] The Pāli literature, moreover, is full of much interesting evidence on the point. The evidence will show that, though normally the trades and crafts were organized on an hereditary basis and technical talent descended from father to son and was confined to a particular family, the way was quite open for exceptions to that rule. Though possibly certain functions were monopolized by the Brahmans and the political functions and offices—except, as we have seen, the office of the king's treasurer (*gahapati*) which was reserved for the

[1] See *Gautama*, VII. 6; *Vasiṣṭha*, II. 22; *Baudhāyana*, II. 4. 16; *Viṣṇu*, II. 15; Manu, X. 81.

merchant-prince—were exercised by both Brahmans and Kṣatriyas, yet members of all classes were free to indulge in the economic pursuits they might affect.

Thus in *Vinaya*, I.77 and IV.128 we find parents discussing the best profession which their son might choose, such as writing,[1] accountantcy,[2] and money-changing[3] without a reference being made to the father's trade. In *Chullavagga*, V. 28 the Bhikkhus are allowed 'the use of a loom and of shuttles, strings, tickets, and all the apparatus belonging to a loom'. The Jātakas mention many instances of different degrees of intimacy between the Brahmans, burghers, and princes, and even the lower classes, culminating even in intermarriages or sending sons to the same teacher for education [*Jāt.* I. 421, 422[4]; III. 9–11,[5] 249–54,[6] 340,[7] 405,[8] 406, 475[9];

[1] *Lekhaṃ.* [2] *Gaṇanaṃ.*

[3] *Rūpaṃ*, i. e. money-changing, which will affect the eyes (*akkhīnī dukkhā bhavissanti*). Cf. Buddhaghosa's note quoted in *S. B. E.*, vol. xiii, p. 201: 'He who learns the *rūpa-sutta* must turn over and over many *kārṣāpaṇas* and look at them.'

[4] A king marries a rustic woman on account of her decency.

[5] A king being defeated by rebels finds a hospitable shelter with a poor countryman, and rewards his benefactor with the half of his kingdom.

[6] A king marries an ascetic's daughter.

[7] There is a marriage between a queen and her priest's son.

[8] The Kosala king, being defeated by Ajātasatru, escapes to a forest where he sees the daughter of the chief of the garland-makers of Sāvatthi.

[9] 'Once upon a time, when Brahmadatta was reigning in

IV. 38[1]; VI. 348,[2] 421, 422[3]]. The free love of the times expressed itself in the following strain: 'Whomsoever the lover loves, be it a low Chaṇḍālī, all are alike: in love there is no unlikeness'; and again, 'The mother of the king of Sivi is named Jambāvati (of the Chaṇḍāla caste), and she was the beloved queen consort of Vāsudeva, one of the Kaṇhāgana clan' [*Jāt.* 421]. We also read of Brahmans[4] as physicians [IV. 361], goat-herds [III. 401], merchants, hunters, snake-charmers [IV. 457], archers, and the servant of an archer who was formerly a weaver [III. 219; V. 127, 128; I. 356, 357], low-caste trappers (*nesādā*) [II. 200: VI. 170]; even cartwrights [IV. 207, 208]. In *Jāt.* III. 49–51, a deer-trapper (*migaluddaka*) becomes the protégé and then the inseparable companion of a rich young seṭṭhi. In *Jāt.* V. 290–3 a kṣatriya, a king's son, named Kusa, in his infatuation for Pabhāvatī, apprentices himself incognito in succession to the court potter, basket-maker, florist, and cook to his

Benares, his son, young Brahmadatta, and young Mahādhana, son of a rich merchant of Benares, were comrades and play-fellows, and were educated in the same teacher's house.'

[1] The son of a poor woman of a caravan, a merchant's son, and the son of a tailor in the employ of the merchant, 'all grew up together, and by and by went to Takkāsila to complete their education'.

[2] A Brahman's daughter is married by the king.

[3] Instances of intermarriage between castes in traditional stories.

[4] *Jātaka*, no. 495, gives a long list of the various occupations followed by Brahmans.

father-in-law without a word being said as to his loss of caste when these vagaries became known. In *Jāt.* IV. 84 a prince takes to trade, while in IV. 169 another resigning his kingdom goes to the frontier where he dwells 'with a rich merchant's family, working with his own hands'.

We have in our literature even some examples of king-craftsmen,[1] showing that in those days the practice of a craft was not considered derogatory to the dignity of a prince. The *Kusa-Jātaka* [no. 531], for instance, mentions a prince who only consents to marry when a princess is found exactly like a golden image which he himself had fashioned and which was far superior to that made by the chief smith employed for the purpose. A more historical example of a royal craftsman is king Jetthatissa of Ceylon, referred to in the *Mahāvamsa* as a 'skilful carver and painter who wrought a beautiful image of the Bodhisatta and also a throne, a parasol, and a state-room with beautiful work in ivory made for it, and who himself taught the arts to his subjects'. In Bāna's *Harsha Charita* it is stated how on the occasion of the marriage of a princess 'even kings girt up their loins and busied themselves in carrying out decorative work set as tasks by their sovereign'.

Thus all the evidence shows that at the times

[1] Manu, VII. 43 lays down that the king must learn 'from the people the trades and professions'. [वार्त्तारम्भांश्च लोकतः ।]

to which it relates the division of castes was not quite rigid and was no bar to the free mobility of labour both vertical and horizontal. Social divisions and economic occupations were very far from coinciding. There was, of course, plenty of pride of birth (which discouraged interdining and intermarrying between certain ranks) and sons, especially among artisans, tended to follow the paternal industry. Thus individuals and also families are often referred to in terms of their traditional calling [*M. Par. Sutta* 40[1]; *Jat.* I. 98[2]; 194,[3] 312[4]; II. 79[5]; III. 376[6]]. But, as we have seen, so far from their being any exclusiveness in ordinary intercourse between nobles, priests, and commoners, who were making or had made fortunes in trade, we frequently find the sons of burghers the playmates and schoolfellows of princes and young Brahmans. Thus the recognition of the dignity of all labour was a levelling

1 'How delightful a spot, Ānanda, is Vesāli, and the *Udena* chetiya, and the *Gotamaka* chetiya, and the *Sattambaka* chetiya, and the *Bahuputta* chetiya, and the *Sārandada* chetiya, and the *Chāpāla* chetiya.'

2 'The Bodhisatta was born into a merchant's family, and growing up in due course used to journey about *trading*.'

3 'A *young* merchant.'

4 'Chittahattha-Sāriputta.'

5 The Bodhisatta born as a potter's son plied the potter's trade.

6 The Bodhisatta born in a potter's family followed the potter's handicraft. For other references see *Jāt.* II. 30, 302; III. 286, 508; IV. 251; VI. 26, 336.

influence promoting a social equality and brotherhood which subdued the pride of caste.

There were, however, certain notable exceptions to this principle of the equality of social status of various crafts. Thus there were recognized certain low tribes or castes (*hīna-jātiyo*) and low trades or crafts (*hīna-sippa*). As instances of low castes are mentioned the *Nesādas*, hunters or trappers [*Ab.* 518, 1038; *Pāt.* 83[1]] the *Chaṇḍālas* who are called 'the lowest race that go upon two feet—meanest men on earth' [*Jāt.* IV. 397], contact with whom was pollution [*Jāt.* II. 83; III. 233; IV. 376], who lived apart in their own settlements [*Jāt.* IV. 200, 376] by hunting and sometimes by street-sweeping, [*Jāt.* IV. 390] and policing towns by night [*Jāt.* III. 30]; and the *Pukkusas*[2] whose occupation is said to be that of throwing away dead flowers [*Ab.* 508; *Jāt.* IV. 205[3]]. As examples of low crafts are mentioned those of the *Veṇas*, workers in bamboo or wicker-work [*Ab.* 509; *Pāt.* 83[3]], wheel-wrights and carriage-builders (*ratha-kāras*), basket-makers, potters, weavers, leather-workers, and barbers, all called *hīna sippa* in the list given in the *Sutta-*

[1] See Childers.

[2] According to Manu the son of a Niṣāda by a Śūdra female becomes a Pukkasa by caste [IV. 18], his occupation is that of catching and killing animals living in holes [X. 49]. Cf. *Viṣṇu*, XVI. 9: 'Pukkasas must live by hunting.' See also Childers.

[3] See Childers.

Vibhanga [See *Vin.* IV. 6–10[1]; (M. II. 152; A. II. 85=P.P. 51; S. I. 73;) *Jāt.* IV. 413[2] V. 337[3]. It should, however, be noted that the social stigma resting on these 'low trades' was due sometimes to their very nature (as in the case of butchering, for example) but chiefly to their association with the aboriginal non-Aryan tribes who followed them as their hereditary occupations. It is also a significant fact that the same stigma attached to the 'hireling' working with another man's capital and for his profits, for in a list of callings given in the Buddhist books he ranks along with the mere hewers of wood and flower-gatherers and below the slave [see D. I. 51; *Mil.* 147, 331; A. I. 145, 206; II. 67[4]. The slave was indeed better treated; the only case of slave-beating is that of a slave-girl let out to work for hire but returning home without her wage [*Jāt.* I. 402, 403]. In *Jāt.* I. 390 the conversion of free peasant proprietors into hirelings, toiling on the estates of the royal capitalist,[5] with 'their own

[1] 'Hīnaṃ nāma sippaṃ nalakārasippaṃ kumbhakārasippaṃ pesakārasippam chammakārasippam nahāpitasippaṃ.' Among the *hīnajāti* or low castes the *Vinaya* enumerates the chaṇḍāla, veṇa, nesāda, rathakāra, and pukkusa.'

[2] 'A village of hunters near Benares' is mentioned.

[3] 'A village of fowlers' near the city of Sakula, in the kingdom of Mahinisaka, is mentioned.

[4] See *J. R. A. S.*, 1901, p. 862.

[5] *Jāt.* I. 468 gives an instance of a millionaire with his hired labourers.

empty barns at home' is taken to be a sure symptom of social decadence.

Again the *Chullavagga*, XII. 1. 3 mentions as the fourth among 'the four stains by which Samanas and Brahmanas are affected' the practice as 'means of life' of certain 'low arts' which are set out in the *Mahāsīlaṃ* [*Tevigga Sutta*, ch. II] comprising chiefly the black arts, explanation of signs, omens, auguries, dreams, forecasting weather, foretelling events, &c. The *Mil. Panha* [I. 191] seems to attach an indignity to the crafts of 'wrestlers, tumblers, jugglers, actors,[1] ballet-dancers, followers of the mystic cult of the sun and moon, of the goddess of fortune and other gods' who keep the secrets of their craft to their own sect or guild. The *Saddharma-Puṇḍarīka* [ch. III] enjoins that Bodhisattvas and preachers must shun 'chaṇḍālas, jugglers, vendors of pork, poulterers, deer-hunters, butchers, actors and dancers, and wrestlers'. In the *Kula Śīlaṃ* the Bhikkhu is to abstain from dancing, singing, music, and theatrical shows'; in the *Majjhima Śīlaṃ* from all public spectacles (of which a most exhaustive list is given), and from 'performing the servile duties of a go-between, that is to say, between kings, ministers of state, &c.'[2]

[1] *Jāt.* VI. 191 refers to actors as being held in such low repute that no well-bred snake would dance in their presence for shame.

[2] *Jāt.*, no. 179 [II. 82], refers to 'Brethren who used to get a

The 'low-trades' mentioned in the *smṛitis* naturally cover a wider ground because they are determined with reference to the stricter ideals and more orthodox standpoint of the Brāhmaṇa. Yet a comparative consideration of these cannot fail to be interesting for the light it may throw on early Indian social and economic conditions. It will appear from the evidence that there is a substantial agreement between the Pāli works and our law-books in respect of the trades or professions implying an inferior social status. It is not quite pertinent to the present inquiry to refer to certain classes, castes, professions, or peoples, which, according to ancient Hindu law, were subjected to social disapproval on account of their deficiencies due to physical, moral, or religious considerations. From the severe, uncompromising, Puritanic standpoint of the Brahmanical way of life and its austere ideals of inner and outer purity, it is indeed no wonder that serious physical deformities or defects and contagious diseases should render a person unworthy of proper social intercourse, especially on religious occasions like the performance of a *srāddha*; and that a similar disqualification should arise from serious moral delinquencies or breaches of religious

living by being *physicians* (note the prohibition in the Hindu *smṛitis*), or runners, doing errands on foot . . *the twenty-one unlawful callings*'.

rules regarding conduct and discipline proper to the caste to which the offender belonged. But, leaving out of consideration these cases which are peculiar to the Brahmanical system of thought and code of life, we shall find that the crafts and castes, trades and professions on which the Hindu law-books impose a social stigma will be practically identical with those mentioned in the Buddhist books. The Bhikkhu and the Brāhman will indeed appear to have needed the discipline of common regulations and restrictions as regards social intercourse to preserve and protect their respective purity and asceticism. Thus the interdiction of singing, dancing, acting, theatrical performances, and other public spectacles which we find emphasized with such Puritanic rigour in some of the Buddhist books is also similarly repeated in all the important Hindu legal works. Thus Manu condemns *Kuśilavas*, explained by Medhātithi as 'bards, actors, jugglers, dancers, singers, and the like', as being unworthy of invitation at a *srāddha* [III. 155 and 158]; the food given by a musician [IV. 210] and by an actor [IV. 214] is also not acceptable. Among the lowest classes mentioned are *ghallas*, *mallas*, i. e. 'fencers with sticks or wrestlers and jesters' and *nātas*, i. e. stage-players [XII. 45]. Similarly *Vasiṣṭha* condemns actors [III. 3]; also *Baudhāyana* [I. 5. 24] who adds to them stage-players and teachers of dancing, singing, and acting as *upapātakins* [II. 1. 2. 13]. *Nārada* condemns as incompetent witnesses gamesters, dancers, and jugglers [I. 178. 181. 184]. *Bṛihaspati* condemns low artists as no better than thieves [XXII. 3], while *Viṣṇu* holds dancing as a crime [XXXVII. 32], and public dancers [LI. 13] and stage-players [ib. 14] as unworthy of giving food. Similarly the odium attaching to hirelings as mentioned in some of the Buddhist books is confirmed by Hindu law.[1] Thus Manu condemns a paid servant (of a village or a king), temple-priests [III. 152. 153] and domestic priests of kings [XII, 46]. Similarly condemned also are astrologers,[2] weather-prophets,[3] those who interpret evil omens and practise propitiatory rites.[4] The following are the other crafts, professions or occupations[5] on which rests a social stigma, viz. butchers, meat-sellers, bird-fanciers, fowlers, hunters, trappers or poachers (i. e. those who hunt without the bow), *niṣādhas*

[1] In V. 5 Nārada lays down a singular line of distinction between pure and impure occupations: 'Know that there are two sorts of occupations; pure work and impure work. Impure work is that done by slaves. Pure work is that done by labourers.'

[2] Manu, III. 162; *Viṣṇu*, LXXXII. 7; *Nārada*, I. 183.

[3] *Nārada*, I. 183.

[4] *Bṛihaspati*, XXII. 3.

[5] Manu, III. 150–63; IV. 84, 210–16; VIII. 65, 66; XI. 64; XII. 45, 46. *Āpastamba*, I. 6. 14. *Gautama*, XVII. 17. *Vasiṣṭha*, III. 3; XIV. 2, 3. *Baudhāyana*, I. 5. 24; II. 1. 2. 13. *Nārada*, I. 178, 181, 183–85. *Bṛihaspati*, XXII. 3. *Viṣṇu*, XXXVII. 22, 23, 32; LI. 8, 10, 13, 14, 15; LXXXII. 7, 9.

(who live by fishing), trainers of animals (like horses, elephants, camels, oxen), dog-trainers, snake-catchers; leather-manufacturers, cobblers; makers of bows and arrows, dealers in weapons, blacksmiths, goldsmiths; carpenters, weavers, dyers, oil-manufacturers, ploughmen, artisans, mechanics, architects; superintendents or workers in mines or factories; those who execute great mechanical works [1] or make large instruments [2]; washermen, quacks; tailors, shopkeepers, and publicans. It is also interesting to note that Manu, like the Buddhist books, thinks ill of messengers.[3] Basket-makers [4] and workers in cane [5] are also condemned as in the Buddhist works. Gautama bans the police-officer [6] and Vasiṣṭha the mace-bearer,[7] while Nārada [8] brands the enemy of a guild of traders or association of clansmen as unworthy of acceptance as a witness in law-courts. Lastly, the paid priests who sacrifice for a multitude do not escape from their share of the social odium.[9]

[1] Manu, XI. 64: *Mahāyantrapravartana* has been severally explained as 'constructing dams across rivers in order to stop the water' (Medh., Govind., Kulluka); 'making machines for killing great animals such as boars' (Nār.); or 'making great machines such as sugar-mills' (Nand.). Thus mechanical engineers are meant, but it is to be understood that their profession is not approved for a Brāhmaṇa only.

[2] *Viṣṇu*, XXXVII. 23: explained by the commentator 'as instruments for piercing the elephant's ear'.

[3] Manu, III. 163. [4] Manu, IV. 215. [5] *Viṣṇu*, II. 14.

[6] XVII. 17. [7] XIV. 2. [8] I. 184.

[9] Manu, III, 151; *Baudhāyana*, II. 1, 2, 13. As has been

It should of course be carefully borne in mind that the above list of disapproved occupations and 'low trades' is meant only for the guidance of the highest caste in Hindu society, whose special religious duties, social status, privileges, and obligations alone have determined the list without any reference to the other castes, and it is therefore devoid of much economic significance. Thus the aforesaid professions have been disapproved with reference and in relation to two main purposes affecting the Brāhmaṇas, viz. (1) entertainment at a *srāddha* and funeral dinner; (2) receipt of presents or gifts (including food), and in respect of these two purposes the majority of the aforesaid castes and crafts have been declared to be *not* eligible. The principle of the declaration is therefore strictly relative to the religious necessities of a particular caste and does not point to any absolute standard by which the economic functions of society could be regulated.[1] But the principle is meant to be absolute so far as the Brāhmaṇa

already stated, Baudhāyana does not permit the Brāhmaṇa to teach professional dancers, and actors the actual works on their art (*nāṭyāchāryatā*), e. g. the *nāṭya-sūtras* mentioned by Pāṇini.

[1] It is interesting to note that such an absolute standard is laid down by Nārada, V. 5 (already quoted), 6, and 7: 'Sweeping the gateway, the privy, the road, and the place of rubbish; shampooing the secret parts of the body; gathering and putting away the leavings of food, ordure, and urine; and lastly, rubbing the master's limbs when desired; this should be regarded as impure work. *All other work besides this is pure.*'

caste is concerned, for which it certainly defines the sphere of legitimate economic activity—though, however, in the majority of the instances mentioned the principle of disapproval is merely religious and relative to a particular caste, there are some in regard to which the disapproval has perhaps been determined by an absolute and universal standard expressing the social opinion of the whole community. I mean those classes, crafts, or professions which have been condemned as ineligible for the supply of witnesses in suits before law courts. This is no doubt a very limiting regulation and the disqualification accordingly applies but to a few cases. Thus, according to Nārada, only the following are declared to be incompetent witnesses, viz., oil-makers, gamesters, dancers, snake-catchers, ploughmen, weather-prophets, astrologers, jugglers, enemies of guilds, butchers, leather-manufacturers, and quacks [I. 178–85], while Manu limits them down only to three, viz. mechanics, actors, and *dasyus*, which is explained by Medhātithi to mean 'servants for wages' or 'hard-hearted men' and may have meant, as Bühler suggests, 'the aboriginal robber tribes' [VIII. 65]. The contempt for quackery, fraud, and black arts, irrespective of the caste of the person practising them, is indeed remarkable. Manu also, as has been already pointed out, mentions the *ghallas*, *mallas*, *nātas*, and mercenary priests (*cor-*

ruptio optimi pessima) as the *lowest* classes, while Bṛihaspati regards as no better than thieves the quacks, interpreters of evil omens, and practisers of propitiatory rites (mostly Brāhmaṇas) and such low artists. It is thus evident that both the Buddhist and Hindu social opinion is practically at one in condemning certain crafts and professions on the basis of an absolute standard determined on grounds of moral deficiency and in some cases of uncleanliness of the processes of operation involved in the craft or manufacture.[1]

We have now seen, both from the Brahmanical and Buddhist evidence, how far the admission to a craft was affected or restricted by the rules of caste. We shall now proceed to discuss the other features in the organization of craft-guilds.

In the Pāli literature we have many references to apprenticeship but hardly to any terms or conditions regarding the same as we have, for instance, in the

[1] It should be noted in this connexion that along with the aforesaid crafts, manufactures, or professions, there are certain articles or commodities, the trade in which is absolutely forbidden to a Brāhmaṇa. Thus Manu, X. 86–94, specifies among others the following articles: condiments, cooked food, stones, cattle, dyed cloth, cloth of hemp, flax or wool, meat, poison, milk, ghee, oil, perfumes, honey, indigo, lac, sugar, birds, wines, wild animals, weapons, water, &c. Parallel specifications are also contained in *Gautama*, VII. 9–20; *Āpastamba*, I, 7, 20, 12–13: *Baudhāyana*, II. 1, 2, 27; *Vasiṣṭha*, II, 24–32; *Viṣṇu*, LIV, 17–21; *Nārada*, I. 61–6; and *Yājñāvalkya*, III. 36–40.

Nārada-smṛiti. The *Vinaya,* for instance, gives elaborate rules regulating the duties of the *saddhi-vihārika* (pupil) towards his *upajjhāya,* of an *ante-vāsika,* and vice versa, and also rules regulating the *nissaya* or relation between teacher and pupil, and the conditions determining its admissibility or cessation. But these rules relate only to the educa-tion in the sacred lore, religion, and humanities, and not to the training in the crafts with which we are concerned. The apprentice in the industrial sense indeed appears frequently in the Jātaka but no terms or period or other conditions of pupilage are given. Thus in *Jāt.* no. 97 we have a publican and his apprentice, while in *Jāt.* no. 531 [the *Kusa-Jātaka*], as we have already seen, a prince apprentices him-self to a potter, basket-maker, florist, and the royal *chef* in succession. In *Jāt.* V, 457–9, two princes receive instruction in arts at the hands of the same teacher who had besides 101 other pupils. The senior pupil also acts as an assistant teacher (*piṭṭhiā-chariya*). The position of a senior pupil to a *maha-vaddhaki* is indicated by Buddhaghosa [*Asl.* 111. 112]. We have also instances of fees being paid by apprentices to their teachers [*Jāt.* IV. 224. 225; 38. 39, where two merchants' sons paid 2,000 pieces each to their master as fee].

In the Buddhist books the craft-guilds were organized under a head called *pamukha* or *jeṭṭaka* but there is one instance, as we have already seen, of all the guilds having a common chief, who was also lord of the treasury in the kingdom of Kāsi. The centralization in this case was perhaps due to quarrels between the foremen of the subordinate guilds such as those at Sāvatthi mentioned in *Jāt.* II. 12. 52.

There seems to have been also a considerable localization of trades and crafts. Suburban villages grew up to serve the cities where certain crafts were exclusively localized; e.g. smith villages of 1,000 families [*Jāt.* III. 281–6]; villages of wood-wrights numbering 500 [*Jāt.* II. 18. 405; IV. 208] and sometimes towns [*Jāt.* IV. 159] containing 1,000 families; and villages famous for potters [*Jāt.* III. 376. 508]. There were also crafts localized in special quarters of the cities; e.g. the ivory-workers' bazaar in the city of Benares [*Jāt.* I. 320; II. 197], dyers, perfumers, and florists [*Jāt.* IV. 81. 82]; the cooks' quarters in Sāvatthi [*Jāt.* III. 48; sometimes the crafts were associated with special streets named after them in the cities; e.g. the washermen's-street [*Jāt.* IV. 81] in Asitañjanā, the Vaisya-street and quarter [*Jāt.* VI. 485].

We have also some evidence of localization of trades and industries in Sanskrit works. The *Kauṭilīya* [II. 1] refers to the artificial creation by the king of villages of agriculturists belonging to the

Sūdra caste, of Brāhmaṇa villages and forests for their undisturbed pursuit of learning and religion, of mines and factories, timber and elephant forests and markets. Within the city the various trades and crafts were localized in special quarters and their distribution followed a definite plan. Thus every caste and craft had a locality of its own [see II. iv. for the details of the distribution]. In the Śilpa śāstra work called *Mānasāra* is described a village plan called *Nandyāvarta* meant for a mixed population of different social grades assigned to different localities. There is an example of village-planning mentioned in a South Indian inscription of the thirteenth century A.C. in which the village is intended to accommodate 108 Brahman families with lands for grazing cattle, new settlers and remuneration of the village officers and artisans [*Madras Epigraphy, Annual Report*, 1913–14, p. 92]. One of the Ukkal inscriptions mentions villages of Brāhmaṇas, of Vaikhānasas and of Śramaṇas (i. e. Jainas) in the Chola, Tondai and Pāndya countries [no. 9, Hultzsch, *S. I. Inscr.*, vol. III, p. 15].

The control of the guild over its members is evident from the fact that it was entitled to arbitrate on certain occasions between its members and their wives [*Vin.* IV. 226] and also from the ordinance of the Buddhist church, which forbade the giving religious orders to the wife of a member unless his guild had sanctioned it [*Sutta Vibhanga* quoted in *Economic Journal*, 1901. p. 313].

Merchant-guilds do not seem to have attained the same development as the craft-guilds. The reason seems to be that the merchant was necessarily a wanderer, while industrial organizations depend largely on the circumstance of neighbourhood. A Hansa League, for instance, can only grow in highly developed markets and at sea-ports. Nevertheless there is some significant evidence of corporate, concerted action among the merchants: the *Chullakaseṭṭhi* Jātaka mentions a hundred or so of merchants offering to bring up a newly-arrived ship's cargo [*Jāt.* I. 122]; 500 traders were fellow-passengers on board the ill-fated ships mentioned in *Jāt.* II. 128; 700 others were lucky enough to secure Suppāraka as their pilot [*Jāt.* IV. 138–42], thus showing co-operative chartering of the same vessel. Again, caravan-traders had their chief who was to give directions as to halts, watering, precautions against robbers, and, in many cases, as to route, fords, &c. [*Jāt.* I. 98. 99. 107. 174; II. 295. 335; III. 200]. Further, several partnerships are mentioned, e.g. in a deal in birds exported from India to Babylon [*Jāt.* III. 126. 127], in horses imported from the 'north' to Benares [*Jāt.* II. 31], partnerships of traders of Sāvatthi who carried on joint-business and set out with 500 cart-loads of merchandise [*Jāt.* IV.

350–4]; of two other traders of Sāvatthi who 'joined partnership and loaded 500 waggons full of wares' [*Jāt.* II. 181]; partnership business in pots and pans [*Jāt.* I. 111]; partnership of two merchants of Benares who 'took 500 waggons of merchandise from Benares to the country-districts' with an equal interest of both in the 'stock-in-trade and in the oxen and waggons' [*Jāt.* I. 404]. A concerted commercial enterprise on a more extensive scale appears in *Jāt.* II. 294–6, where some traders in Sāvatthi carried on joint business and came upon rich finds of 'minerals of all sorts from iron to lapis lazuli', which they stowed away in a common treasure-house, giving food to the brotherhood on joint account. These are distinguished from another partnership of traders who were more greedy and came to grief. Again, *Jāt.* II. 248 shows concerted action in work and play of 'certain traders in Benares who made a journey to Ujjeni for trade', where they afterwards gave themselves up to merry-making.

The existence of a merchant-guild ruling the trade of the city of Sopara is mentioned in the legend of Pūrna, translated by Burnouf from Nepalese and Tibetan sources apparently of the third or fourth century B.C. [*Bombay Gazetteer*, old ed., vol. XIII, p. 406]

Partnerships are known to the *smṛiti* works of Nārada and Bṛihaspati, which lay down the laws regulating them. The loss, expenses, and profits of the business are to be shared by each partner according to the share contributed by him to the joint-stock[1] [*Nārada*, III. 1. 3–4[2]; *Bṛihaspati*, XIV. 3–4[3]]. The charges or expenses of business include those for stores, food, tolls, freight, losses, &c. [*Nārada*, III. 4[2]]. A partner is responsible for any loss due to his want of care or any action without the assent, or against the instructions of his co-partners [*Nārada*, III. 5[4]; *Bṛihaspati* XIV. 9].[5] Similarly, he is entitled to a special remuneration for special profit gained through his individual action [*Nārada*, III. 6[6]; *Bṛihaspati*, XIV. 10[7]]. A con-

[1] Cf. Manu, VIII. 211; *Yājñāvalkya*, II. 259.

[2] वाणिक् प्रभृतयो यत्र कर्मसंभूयकुर्वते तत्संभूयसमुत्थानं व्यवहारपदंस्मृतम् समोऽतिरिक्तो हीनोवा तत्रांशोयस्ययाद्दृशः क्षयव्ययौ तथावृद्धिस्तच तस्यतथाविधाः भाण्डपिण्डव्ययोद्धार भारसारान्ववेक्षणम् कुर्युस्तेऽव्यभिचारेण समये स्वेव्यवस्थिताः।

[3] समोन्यूनोऽधिकोवांशोयेन क्षिप्तस्तथैव सः।
व्ययं दद्यात्कर्म्म कुर्य्याल्लाभं गृह्णीत चैवहि॥
प्रयोगं कुर्व्वतेयेतु हेमधान्यरसादिना।
समन्यूनाधिकैरंशैर्लाभस्तेषां तथाविधः॥

[4] प्रमादान्नाशितं दाप्यः प्रतिषिद्धकृतं चयत्।
असंदिष्टश्च यत्कुर्यात्सर्वसंभूयकारिभिः॥

[5] अनिर्दिष्टो वार्य्यमाणः प्रमादाद्यस्तु नाशयेत्।
तेनैव तद्भवेद्देयं सर्व्वेषां समवायिनाम्॥

[6] दैवतस्कररराजाग्निव्यसने समुपस्थिते।
यस्तत्स्वशक्त्या रक्षत्तु तस्यांशोदशमः स्मृतः॥

[7] राजदैवभयाद्यस्तु स्वशक्त्या परिपालयेत्।
तस्यांशं दशमं दत्त्वा गृह्णीयुस्तेऽशतोऽपरम्॥

tract executed by one is binding on all [*Bṛihaspati* XIV. 5].[1]

§ 2

The epigraphic evidence also confirms the literary evidence and throws some new light on these organizations of craft-guilds and merchant-guilds. We read of munificent religious endowments and benefactions executed by merchant princes and prosperous guilds whose wealth is derived from success in trade and commerce. The great *chaitya* cave at Karli was the gift of a śeṭh (*śreṣṭhin*) of Vaijayanti. There were similar costly gifts at other places also, such as those at Kanhery. In the Mathura Jaina image inscription (no. 24 in Lüders's List)[2] the wife of the śreṣṭhi Veṇi dedicates a four-fold image of Bhagavāna. Similarly in the Mathurā Jaina elephant capital inscription of the time of Mahārājā Devaputra Huviṣka the elephant Nandi-viśāla is set up by the śreṣṭhi Ārya Rudradāsa for the worship of the Arhats [no. 41]. In the inscriptions of Sānchi stūpa assigned to the period dating from Asoka's time up to the first century A. C. [*Ep. Ind.*, vol. II, p. 88] we have records of gifts made by several merchants, viz. those of Sāma-

[1] बहूनांसम्मतोयस्तु दद्यादेको धनं नरः ।
करणं कारयेद्वापि सर्व्वैरेव कृतं भवेत् ॥

[2] *Ep. Ind.*, vol. X, App.

nerā, the Abeyaka śeṭh (i.e. 'the śeṭh of a town or village called *Aba* or *Amba*, in Sanskrit *Āmra-grāma*') [no. 184]; of the śeṭh, the great executor of repairs (*patikamakārikānā*) [no. 248]; gift of a pillar (*thava*) by *Nāgapiya*, the Korara (native of Kurāra), a śeṭh in Achhāvaḍa [339]; gift of the śeṭh Śiha [364]; gift of śeṭh Nāgadīna (Nāgadatta), inhabitant of Rohaṇipada [*Ep. Ind.*, vol. II, p. 109]; the gift of Devabhāga, wife of the śeṭh of Kaṁdaḍigrāma [423]; the gift of the śeṭh Nāgila [470]; gift of the śeṭh Budhapālita, native of Padukulikā (Pāṇḍukulikā) [576]; gift of Nāgā, wife of Kaṁdaḍigāmīya śeṭh [no. 140, *Ep. Ind.*, vol. II, p. 372]; of Kaniyasi, the mother of the śeṭh [ibid., no. 167, p. 374]; of Kujara (Kuñjara), brother of the śeṭh [ibid., no. 170, p. 375]; of Nāgapiya, the śeṭh of Achhāvada and of his son Saṁgha [ibid., no. 201, p. 378]. The inscription no. 190 in Cunningham, *Bhilsa Topes* [p. 264] records the gift of Ānaṁda, the son of Vāsiṭhi (Vāsiṣṭhi), the foreman of the artisans (*āvesanin*) of Rājā Siri-Sātakaṇi. Some of the Kanhery Buddhist cave inscriptions record gifts of artisans and merchants. No. 986 in Lüders's List mentions the gift of a cistern (*pāniyaka*) by a goldsmith, Samidata of Kaliyāna. No. 987 mentions the building of a *chaitya* by the merchants (*vāṇijaka*) of which the overseers included a merchant (*negama*) named Aparenuka, while the labourers included the stonecutters (*sela-vadhakin*), the *nāyakamisas*, the *kadhi-chakas*, the *mahākaṭakas* and the polisher (*mīṭhika*) Khadaraki. No. 995 mentions the gift of a cistern (*poḍhī*) of the merchant (*negama*) Samika from Sopāraga (*Śūrpāraka*). No. 998 mentions the gift of a cave (*leṇa*), a water-cistern (*pāṇiyapoḍhī*), benches for sitting on (*āṣaṇapeḍhikā*), a chair (? *pidha*) and a walk (*chakama*) by the merchant (*negama*), Dhama. No. 1,000 mentions the gift of a cave and cistern by a merchant named Isipāla; no. 1,001 of a cave by a merchant; no. 1,005 of a cave by a jeweller (*manikara*), Nāgapālita of Sūrpāraka; no. 1,024 the gift of a cave, and a hall (*koḍhi*) by Aparēṇu the son of a Kalyāṇa merchant; and no. 1,032 the gift of a path (? *patha*) by the blacksmith (Kamāra) Nada (Nanda) from Kalyāṇa. Nos. 1,202, 1,203, and 1,204 record gift of five entrance pillars to the Great Chaitya of Velagiri by the foreman of a guild of artisans named Sidhatha (*āvesani*). No. 1,298 [Amarāvatī inscription] mentions another foreman Nadabhuti (Nandabhūti). In the Kudā Buddhist cave inscriptions [nos. 1,063, 1,064] we have the gifts of a cave by the *śeṭhin* Vasulaṇaka and of a cistern (*poḍhī*) by the same śeṭh. In the Mahāḍ Buddhist cave inscription [1073] we have the gift of a cave (*leṇa*) and a chaitya hall (*chetiakoḍhi*) by the wife of the śeṭh Saṁgharakhita and in the Kol Buddhist cave inscription [1075] the gift of a cave by the śeṭh of the same name. In the Karle Buddhist cave inscription [*Ep. Ind.*, vol. VII, p. 48] we have the establishment of a cave-dwelling (*śelaghara*) the most excellent one in Jambudvīpa, by the śeṭh Bhutapāla from Vejayaṁtī (Vaijayanti), or Banavāsi in the North Kanara district. The Beḍsā Buddhist cave inscription [1,109] mentions the gift of Pusaṇaka (Puṣya), son of the śeṭh Ānada from Nāsika. The Amarāvati Buddhist sculpture inscription [1,261] records the gift of a rail bar (*suchi*) by the righteous hamlet (*bhadanigama*), the Chadakicha (of Chadaka), headed by the śeṭhs.

But besides these instances of gifts of individual merchant-princes, heads of families or aldermen and foremen of villages and guilds we have also instances of collective donations made by villages, towns, and guilds. Thus the Bharhut Buddhist coping-stone inscription [Cunningham, *Stūpa of Bharhut*, no. 16, p. 131] records a gift of the town (*nigama*) of Karahakaṭa. Out of about 285 votive inscriptions of the Sānchi stupa there are ten recording donations by corporate bodies or families. Among these may be mentioned those made by the Vejaja village (*gāma*) [*Ep. Ind.*, vol. II, no. 17, p. 98] and Pāḍukulikā village [ibid., no. 1 of Tope II, p. 110]; the gift of the *Bodhagoṭhi* (*Bauddhagoṣṭhi*) of Dharma vardhanana [ibid., nos. 25, 26, pp. 99, 100], a *goṣṭhi* being 'a committee of trustees in charge of a temple or of a charitable foundation' [Bühler, ibid., p. 92]; of the Barulamisa *goṭhi* from Vedisa [ibid., no. 51, p. 102]. The Sānchi Stūpa inscription, no. 200 [ibid., p. 378], mentions that the carving (*rūpa kamma*) was done by the workers in ivory of Vedisa who had organized themselves into a guild (*śreṇī*) and made that collective gift, as suggested by Bühler [ibid., p. 92]. Among the gifts made by clans or families we have those made by the *Vākiliyas* of Ujjain [ibid., no. 27, p. 100] and the relatives of the venerable *Nāgila* [ibid., no. 84, p. 106].

The Junnar Buddhist cave inscription [no. 10, Bühler-Burgess, *Arch. Surv. W. Ind.*, vol. IV., p. 94] records the gift of a seven-celled cave (*satagabha*) and a cistern (*poḍhī*) by the guild (*śeṇī*) of corn-dealers (*dhaṁññika*).

Some of the Bhattiprolu inscriptions which, according to Bühler, are 'not later than 200 B.C.', record gifts made by *goṭhi's* or committees [*Ep. Ind.*, vol. II, p. 325]. Thus no. 3 mentions the names of the members of the *goṭhi*. No. 6 mentions the gift of a casket (*majūsa*), the crystal-box (*shamuga*) and the stone-box (*shamuga*) by 'the members of the Shāgaṭhi guild or town (*nigama*) chief among whom is the king who was Khubiraka, the chief of the Ṣīha (*Ṣiṁha*) *goṭhi*'. The members of the guild are named in no. 8.

In the Mandasor inscription of Kumāragupta and

Bandhuvarman [Fleet, *Gupta Inscriptions*, p. 86] it is stated how 'a noble and unequalled temple of the bright-rayed sun was caused to be constructed by the silk-cloth weavers as a guild with the stores of wealth acquired by the exercise of their craft' in the city of Daśapura under king Bandhuvarman. Afterwards under other kings part of this temple fell into disrepair. And then it was restored by the *same* guild, showing that this particular guild had quite a long life. It is also stated that this guild of silk-cloth weavers had emigrated from their native district and after various vicissitudes of fortune prospered sufficiently to be able to pay the cost of building that temple. Some of these weavers are also stated to have taken to other trades. This shows once again the mobility of labour and the elasticity of occupations.[1]

In the Indor copper-plate inscription of Skandagupta [ibid., p. 71] a gift is recorded of a Brāhmaṇa who endowed a temple of the sun and transferred the temple-properties to a guild of local oil-men of the town of Indrapura on two conditions, viz. (1) that the guild should continue in complete internal concord and (2) that the guild should make

[1] 'In A.D. 437 a colony of silk-weavers that had emigrated from Lāṭa or Southern Gujrat to Daśapura—now Dasor or Mandasor in Mālava—built there a temple of the sun and in A.D. 473 the same guild restored it' [Burgess, *Arch. Survey*, *W. Ind.*, vol. IX, p. 73].

a permanent arrangement to supply the temple daily with 'two palas of oil'. If these two conditions were observed, even the withdrawal of the donees from that place would not deprive them of the possession of those properties.

It is interesting to find that very similar gifts are also recorded in some of the later South Indian inscriptions. A common form of pious offering consisted in the dedication of a lamp, i.e. providing for a continuous supply of oil or *ghī* for a lamp to be constantly burning before the image in the temple. In some of the Tanjore inscriptions we have mention of guilds of shepherds arranging it on receipt of the required sum of money or its equivalent value in sheep or cattle from the donor. The cost of thus maintaining one sacred lamp was 96 ewes, or 48 cows, or 16 she-buffaloes. 'The shepherds who received the cattle, themselves and their people, viz. their relations and the relations of the latter, had to supply *ghī* to the treasury of the Lord, as long as the sun and moon endures, at the daily rate of one *urakku* of *ghī* . . . for each sacred lamp' [Hultzsch, *South Indian Inscriptions*, vol. II, part III, p. 251]. Quite in accordance with the obligations of partnership indicated above, we find in another inscription[1] of Rājendra Choladeva at Tanjore an

[1] No. 18 in vol. II, part I, of Hultzsch, *South Indian Inscriptions*.

agreement by which the entire guild binds itself to a contract executed on its behalf by an individual member of the guild for the supply of oil in perpetuity for a sacred lamp, The inscription runs as follows: 'We, all the following shepherds of this village . . . agreed to become security for Eran Sattan, a shepherd of this village, (who) had received 90 ewes of this temple in order to supply *ghī* for burning one perpetual lamp. We shall cause the shepherd Eran Sattan to supply daily to one perpetual lamp one *ulakku* of *ghī*. . . . If he dies, absconds, or gets into prison, fetters (or) chains, we, all these aforesaid persons, are bound to supply *ghī* for burning the holy lamp as long as the sun and moon endure.' The inscription gives the name of the local merchant also who may have been the donor of the lamp. The legal phraseology of the inscription is worthy of a modern corporate body, exhausting, as it does, the various conditions under which the responsibility of the guild is acknowledged. The length of the term contemplated for the contract shows the longevity of the institution surviving the death of particular individual members and continuing its collective life throughout the changes in its personnel. It also appears that the guild served as a bank for the community, holding as trust-properties the religious benefactions of individuals who are assured of the permanent and perpetual contribution of their pious offering and worship by the comparatively immortal character of these institutions.

Thus the guilds in their capacity as banks served to stimulate spiritual benefactions and pious gifts in the community. Their religious uses indeed seem to have been universally appreciated and taken advantage of. We have several inscriptions in Northern India to prove this. No. 12 of the Nasik Cave inscriptions, assigned by Burgess to the time of the last Mauryas or the earliest Suṅgas (about second century B.C.), records how Uṣavadāta, son-in-law of king Nahapāna, 'has bestowed this cave on the *saṁgha* generally; he has also given a perpetual endowment, three thousand—3,000—*kāhāpaṇas*, which, for the members of the *saṁgha* of any sect and any origin dwelling in this cave, will serve as cloth money and money for outside life (*Kuśaṇa*); and those *kāhāpaṇas* have been invested in guilds dwelling at Govadhana, 2,000 in a weavers' guild, interest one *pratika* (monthly) for the hundred (and) 1,000 in another weavers' guild, interest three-quarters of a *paḍika* (monthly) for the hundred; and those *kāhāpaṇas* are not to be repaid, their interest only to be enjoyed . . .' [*Ep. Ind.*, vol. VIII, p. 82]. Here we have a reference to two guilds of weavers which, like banks, received permanent deposits which they held as trust-funds, . the principal of which they were to keep intact and be responsible for, and might invest in their own way subject to that responsibility, as banks do with their deposits, but for the use of that money they had to pay interest at certain stipulated rates to the beneficiary named in the grant—the interest was to be paid to the monks for the purchase of new robes for them at the ceremony of robing held in the month of Śrāvaṇa and for their pocket-money. As the inscription puts it, 'Out of them, the two thousand—2,000— at one *pratika* per cent. are the cloth money; out of them to every one of the twenty monks who keep the *vassa* in my cave, a cloth money of twelve (*kāhāpaṇas*). As to the thousand which has been invested at an interest of three-quarters of a *pratika* (*paḍika*) per cent., out of them the money for *kuśaṇa* (very probably some kind of pocket-money)'. The rates of interest which these guild-banks paid on their fixed deposits were in the one case 12 per cent. per annum and in the other case 9 per cent. which, considering the prevailing rates charged by money-lenders in modern times, especially in rural areas, are not by any means exorbitant. The low rate of the interest in fact is an index at once to the security and stability of the banks, their efficiency, permanence, and prosperity, which attracted to them even royal deposits and benefactions.

Similarly, no. 15 of the Nāsik Series [ibid., p. 89]

records how 'in order to provide medicines for the sick of the *Saṁgha* of monks, of whatever sect and origin dwelling in this monastery on mount Triraśmi, a perpetual endowment has been invested for all time to come with the guilds dwelling (at Govardhana), viz. in the hands of the guild of *Kularikas* (?=*kulāla, potter*), one thousand—1,000—*kārṣāpaṇas*, of the guild of *Odayantrikas* [?=*audayantrika* from *udaya-yantra*, i.e. workers fabricating hydraulic engines], two thousand, of the guild of . . . five hundred—500—of the guild of oilmillers (*tilapiṣaka*). . .'.

One of the Junnar Buddhist cave inscriptions [Bühler–Burgess, *Arch. Surv. W. Ind.*, vol. IV, no. 24, p. 96] records the investment of the income of a field at Vaḍālikā for planting Karañja trees and of another field for planting banyan trees by the lay-worshipper Āḍuthuma, the Śaka, a member of the guild of the Koṇāchikas.

Another inscription of the same series [no. 27] mentions the investment of money with the guild of bamboo-workers (*vasakara*) and the guild of braziers (*Kāsākāra*).

It is, however, remarkable to find that the evidence regarding the guilds of these North Indian inscriptions is confirmed by more numerous South Indian inscriptions. The evidence of the latter is so full of new and interesting details that it is necessary to treat it at some length.

There are several inscriptions in the temples of the village called Tirunamanallur in the South Arcot district assigned to tenth and eleventh centuries of which no less than five supply the evidence we require [*Ep. Ind.*, vol. VII, pp. 132–8]. Thus an inscription of Parantaka I (A.D. 900–940) records the gift of two perpetual lamps with lamp-stands by a servant of his queen who gave for the purpose '90 undying and unaging big sheep' [which implies that 'those sheep which died or ceased to supply milk had to be replaced from among the lambs that had grown up in the meantime' (Hultzsch)], and the gift was placed under the protection of all Māheśvaras. The second records the gift of the queen of Rājādityadeva, son of Parantaka I, of another sacred lamp for which she gave 100 undying and unaging big sheep and a lamp-stand weighing seventy *palam*. The third inscription dated in the seventeenth year of Kannaradeva, i.e. the Rāṣṭrakūṭa king, Kṛṣṇa III, records the gift of a perpetual lamp with lamp-stand by a chief of Milāḍu for which he gave 10 *kalañju* of gold to the village guild, the members of which entered into the following agreement, viz. 'Having received these ten *kalañju* of gold, we, the members of the assembly (*sabhā*) . . . shall have to bring every year 100 *nāli* of ghee and shall have to pour (it) out (i.e. measure it) by the *mādevi* (i.e. a measure called after the chief queen, *mahādevī*) as long as the moon and the sun shall last.' Another inscription, D (in the Śaka year 875) records a similar gift of lamp for which the donor assigned 100 undying and unaging big sheep to the village assembly who 'having received these 100 sheep . . . shall have to pour out ghee to burn as long as the moon and the sun shall last'. The fifth (in the Śaka year 876) records a similar gift of lamp and sheep for which the villagers agree 'to pour out daily one *ulakku* of ghee by the *mādevī*'.

More interesting information is given by another series of inscriptions at Tirukkovalur [ibid., pp. 138–47]. The first, dated in the seventeenth year of Vijaya-Nandivikrama [i.e. of the Gaṅga-Pallava king, Vijaya-Nandivikramavarman (assigned to the ninth century A. C.)], records the gift for one perpetual lamp to the god Perumal (usually Viṣṇu but here Śiva) of the Tiruvīraṭṭānam temple in a village of Malāḍu of '15 *kalañju* of gold which was equal in fineness to the old *kāśu* (designation of some gold coin)' to a guild which entered into the following agreement :—

'We, the citizens of this place, have received these 15 *kalañju* of gold.

Out of the interest of this gold we, the citizens, shall have to pour out daily one *ulakku* of oil.'

Two other inscriptions [B and C] record gifts of 12 *kalañju* of gold 'out of the interest of which' the citizens engage 'to burn one perpetual lamp night and day'. D records a gift of 15 *kalañju* of gold for which the citizens 'shall cause to burn a perpetual lamp night and day at the rate of one *uri* (of oil) per month for each *kalañju*'. This inscription (along with the first) helps us also to ascertain the rate of interest allowed by the village assemblies on the permanent deposit made with them, for it will appear that 15 *kalañju* of gold are expected to yield an income or interest equivalent to the value of 180 *uris* of oil per annum. E and F, however, repeat the gift in kind of the usual number of 100 big sheep perpetually renewed, instead of gold.

H deserves special notice, because it records quite new forms of pious offering and service to the god, because the donor gives 20 *kalañju* of gold 'for bathing the god at every *saṁkrānti*'. The details of the agreement entered into by the guild on receipt of the above deposit were as follows :—

'Having received these 20 *kalañju* of gold, we, the members of the assembly of . . . shall have to supply—at the rate of interest of one *kalam* per *kalañju*—20 *kalam* of paddy by the *perilamai* (measure), cleaning (it), defraying the cooly charge, conveying (the paddy) to the very court-yard of the temple, going (there) and measuring (it).

'To those (temple officials) who shall call for this paddy, we, the members of the assembly of . . . shall have to supply boiled rice after having identified (their) persons.

'The members of the assembly of . . . and the members of the assembly of . . . have to measure 60 *kalam* of paddy by the *perilamai*.

'Having received these (60 *kalam*), (which are equal to) 75 *kalam* by the *kal* of 8 *nāli* [= $\frac{1}{12}$ *kalam* (Hultzsch)], and to 6 *kalam* and three *kuruni* per month . . . twenty (?) pots [evidently required for the bathing of the god which is the purpose of the grant according to l. 2 of the inscription (Hultzsch)].'

I records a gift of 24 sacred lamps to be 'fed by the ghee prepared from the milk' of '2,304 undying unaging big sheep' (the usual rate being 100 sheep to a lamp).

K (assigned to A. D. 1057–58) records a gift of two lamps. 'For feeding these lamps' the donor 'gave 64 undying unaging big cows. From these, one *uri* of *ghee* (has to be supplied) daily to (these) two lamps'. This is indeed a rare instance of a cow being given instead of the usual sheep of the inscriptions.

There are numerous other South Indian inscriptions which contain varieties of information on the subject. We select some of those which contain typical pieces of evidence.

No. 85 [Hultzsch, *South Ind. Inscr.*, vol. I] refers to an 'assembly' (*sabhā*) which made the following written agreement: 'We have received twenty *karañjus*[1] weight of gold. . . . (From) the interest of these 20 *karañjus* of gold, we . . . the great people, who constitute the village-assembly of our village, shall measure and give every year 90 *kāḍis* of paddy, without breaking our promise (even) partially'.[2] Fragment no. 146 [ibid., p. 140] includes as a clause in the agreement the payment of a 'fine of a quarter *pon* daily' for non-fulfilment of the contract.

No. 6 [Hultzsch, *S. Ind. Inscr.*, vol. II, Part I] is a long and interesting inscription recording that Kundavaiyar (daughter of Parāntaka II) deposited certain sums of money (*kāsu*) which were subsequently borrowed on interest by certain village assemblies. The interest had to be paid yearly into the treasury of the Rājarājeśvara temple at Tañjāvur [Tanjore] either in paddy or in money. In the former case the interest was three *kuruṇi* of paddy for each

[1] A *karañju* contains 20 *mañjāḍis*, 1 *mañjāḍi* contains 2 *kunris*, and 1 *kunri* is equal to about 2 grains [Hultzsch, *S. Ind. Inscr.*, vol. I, p. 116].

[2] We may compare with this no. 176 of 1915 of Rājendra-Chola I where the gold coin *kāśu* is stated to be equivalent to 3 *kalañju* fetching an interest of 9 *mañjāḍi* per year, interest at 15 per cent. per annum (taking 1 *kalañju* = 20 *mañjāḍi*). It is also stated that paddy was sold at 40 *kāḍi* per *kalañju*. In the inscription no. 245 of 1915, about 20 years later, it appears that the rate of interest nearly trebled itself as 7½ *kalañju*, and 2 *mañjāḍi* fetched an interest of 3 *kalañju* and 8 *mañjāḍi*. The rate of exchange in paddy was 13½ *kalams* per *kalañju*.

kāśu, and in the latter 12½ per cent. ['12 *akkam* being reckoned as one *kāśu* . . . one eighth *akkam* per month should be paid as interest for each *kāśu*' (paragraph 20 of the inscription)]. If it is assumed that the rate of interest was the same in both cases, one *kāśu* would correspond to the value of 24 *kuruṇi* or two *kalam* of paddy.[1] In two instances money was deposited for purchasing a number of the usual sheep from the milk of which a certain amount of ghee for lamps was to be supplied. The value of one sheep was reckoned as ⅓ *kāśu* (one *urakku* of ghee being obtained from 76 sheep bought for 32 *kāśus* to keep 10 twilight lamps burning).

No. 9 [ibid., p. 92] refers to the practice of temple funds being put out at interest to meet the expenses of worship and the rate of interest payable by the guild-banks is the same as no. 6. The same rate of interest on the deposits is repeated in Nos. 10–19.

No. 24 [ibid., Part II, p. 121], records two deposits of money, the first of which is made with 'the great citizens of the great market Tribhuvanamahādevī in Tanjore' who had to supply as interest cardamom seeds and *champaka* buds, and the second with a

[1] According to inscription no. 66 [Hultzsch, *S. Ind. Ins.*, vol. III, p. 136] one *kāśu* purchased about 2¾ *kalam* of paddy. In no. 57, however, we find that 1 *kāśu* corresponds to 4 *kalam* of paddy. This shows that the prices of grain must have varied considerably in different places and times.

No. 80 makes the rate of interest to be as high as 50 per cent.

guild of villagers for supplying *khaskhas* roots. These three kinds of drugs were used for scenting the bathing-water of the temple-gods. The rate of interest is the usual rate stated in the previous records.

No. 25 mentions a new kind of pious offering to the temple. A deposit is made with a village, the interest of which is to ensure the beat of drum at certain festivals.

No. 26 requires the interest of the deposit to be paid in paddy and to be used for procuring various articles of consumption on 13 yearly provision days, and the interest of a second deposit to be paid in cash for purchasing camphor to be burnt before the images.

No. 27 requires the interest to be spent on camphor, also 'to be burnt instead of the wick in one perpetual sacred lamp'.

No. 28 requires the interest on the deposit to be used for feeding 10 Śiva-yogins on each of 24 festival days.

No. 35 records a deposit with 'a free village' of which the interest was to be paid in paddy.

No. 37 records a deposit with four markets (*bāẓārs*) at Tanjore, which had to pay the interest in the shape of a daily supply of a fixed number of plantains for the god.

No. 1 [Hultzsch, *S. Ind. Inscr.*, vol. III, part I]

records that a certain Brahmādhirāja deposited 200 *kalañju* of gold with the village assembly, which pledged itself to apply the interest of this sum to the feeding of 12 learned Brāhmaṇas, their dietary consisting of 1 *ālākku* of ghee, 5 dishes of curry, 2 areca-nuts, and betel-leaves.

No. 5 (ibid., p. 9) records the transfer of 1,000 *kāḍi* of paddy to the village assembly of Uṭkar, who pledged themselves to supply in return 500 *kāḍi* of paddy per year. Thus the deposit as well as the interest was paid in kind.

No. 6 mentions a village assembly assigning a daily supply of rice and oil to a temple.

No. 10 (ibid., p. 15) records that the village assembly of Ukkal sold 3,000 *kuli* of land and 5 water-levers to a servant of the king who assigned this land for the maintenance of two boats plying on the village tank.[1]

No. 14 (ibid., p. 21) records a cultivation gift of some land from the proceeds of which the village assembly had to supply water and fire-pans, and to construct a water-lever in front of the cistern at a *maṇḍapa* frequented by Brāhmaṇas.

No. 28 (ibid., p. 57) mentions a village assembly

[1] A gift of two water-levers (*jala-yantra*) is recorded in the Udayendiram plates of Pallavamalla [ibid., vol. II, pp. 364 and 372]. One of the Nāsik inscriptions states that Ṛṣabhadatta established boats on which certain rivers could be crossed gratuitously [*Arch. Surv. W. Ind.*, vol. IV, p. 100].

receiving on interest 100 *kāśu* from a temple and 'giving against the interest accruing from these 100 *kāśu*' 2,200 *kuli* of land in exchange.

No. 31 (ibid., p. 73) records the gift of land and 'the gold necessary for making the land tax-free' to a village assembly in order to provide processions on new-moon days out of its produce.

No. 44 (ibid., p. 96) records that a Brāhmaṇa paid 25 *kalañju* of gold to an assembly who pledged themselves to supply oil to a lamp in the temple, or, in case of default, to pay into court a fine of five *kalañju* of gold per day. A gift of 20 *kalañju* of gold for a similar purpose and on similar conditions is granted in no. 46.

No. 47 (ibid., p. 100) repeats the same gift and conditions and the fine with the addition that, 'though fined the assembly shall (continue) to supply the ghee without fail'. No. 48 does the same for one camphor lamp and a perpetual lamp.

No. 64 (ibid., p. 134) introduces a new form of pious offering. An assembly sells for 240 *kāśu* a piece of land dedicated to the expenses of anointing the god.

No. 83 (ibid., p. 202) records the rare instance of a gift of 12 cows for the supply of three *ulakku* of ghee and 1 *nāli* of curds 'for offerings on those holy Sundays on which the god is carried outside for the *śrībali*'.

No. 85 (ibid., p. 209) records the gift of 32 cows for a lamp.

§ 3

Without multiplying further instances, those already adduced will make it quite clear that both North Indian and South Indian evidence agree remarkably in attributing to the guilds or assemblies banking functions which were taken full advantage of by the public in making permanent religious endowments. Secondly, we have seen that according to both northern and southern evidence the deposits with the banks were made under proper deeds of agreement reciting the conditions under which they were held. In the concluding part of the Nāsik inscription cited above [no. 8, *Ep. Ind.*, vol. VIII, p. 83] we have the following sentence: 'And all this has been proclaimed (and) registered at the town-hall, at the record office, according to custom'. This suggests a double formality: first, the notification (*śrāvita*) of the gift, and, secondly, its registration (*nibadha*). The endowment was recorded in the archives conformably to rule. But with regard to these legal details and formalities of the transactions the South Indian evidence is at once more abundant and explicit as we have already seen. It also introduces us to certain new and interesting features regarding the religious benefactions. In the first place these were, from the nature of the case, mostly for Hinduism rather than for Buddhism or Jainism. Secondly, the purposes of the grants were both sacred and secular. In the northern inscriptions we have also two instances of the endowments being applied for the robes, pocket-money, and medicines of the monks, and of another for a perpetual sacred lamp. In the southern inscriptions we have several instances of endowments being offered for the support of Brāhmaṇas in the place of the Buddhist monks of the northern, while, as regards sacred purposes, we have many varieties of the same recorded, besides provision of the permanent lamp, viz., food for gods, anointing, processions on festival days, camphor lamps, beat of drum at festivals, scents for the bathing-water of the gods, and the like. We have also two remarkable examples of secular charity, viz., provision of free ferry boats in a village tank, and of water, fire-pans, and a water-lever to a cistern for a Brāhmaṇa settlement. Thirdly, the South Indian epigraphic evidence points to the extensive practice of making payments of charities in kind according to the convenience of the donors and also of the receivers of those trust-properties. The majority of the instances represents payment of the necessary value of the charity in sheep, but we find also a few instances of the payment in cows. There are many cases of payment in land or villages. Fourthly, the rate of interest allowed on these religious deposits was not quite uniform. In some cases it was $12\frac{1}{2}$ per cent., and in a few others as much as 50 per cent. The rate of interest in the northern inscriptions seems to have been slightly lower. Lastly, it should be observed that the South Indian religious endowments were mostly assigned or entrusted to village corporations, the scope of whose functions and activities seems to have been much wider than that covered by the industrial guilds contemplated in the North Indian inscriptions (of which the precise scope is not ascertainable from the available evidence) and to have embraced the totality of the manifold interests of communal life. We now turn to the methods of administration of that life through the local bodies.

CHAPTER IV

§ I

ADMINISTRATIVE FUNCTIONS

WE have considered the industrial and commercial functions of the ancient Indian local bodies and shall now consider their administrative organization and activities. We have already seen that in our early literature, Vedic, Epic, and Pāli, these local bodies (for convenience termed guilds) already appear as developed institutions, possessed of a distinct organization of their own, claiming and commanding a recognized position of importance and influence in the state. That position, accordingly, we find well-defined in our later legal literature, which recognizes their distinct, and practically independent, political status and also indicates their constitutional relations with the state. If the power of independent legislation is one of the criteria of an independent political status, it is amply fulfilled in the case of these local associations. They developed a distinct body of laws or by-laws to regulate their work and activities, the existence and authority of which are clearly affirmed and admitted by our law-books. Thus Gautama[1] [about 500 B.C.] states [XI. 20]: 'Laws of countries, castes and families which are not opposed to the (sacred) texts have also authority', to which he adds: 'Cultivators, traders, herdsmen, money-lenders, and artisans (have authority to lay down laws) for their respective classes' [XI. 21]. He further states [XI. 22]: 'Having learned the (state of) affairs from those who (in each class) have authority (to speak he shall give) the legal decision'.[2] This means, as Haradatta explains, that the king's legal decision must be given in accordance with that which is declared to be the established law in their community by its authorized and accredited spokesmen and representatives, who are entitled to define it on their behalf. Manu also is quite explicit on the point: 'A king who knows the sacred law must inquire into the laws of castes (*jāti*), and districts or peoples (*jānapada*), guild-laws, and family-laws'[3] [VIII. 41]. Again, 'What may have been practised by the virtuous, by such twice-born men who are devoted

[1] देशजातिकुलधर्माश्चाऽम्नायैरविरुद्धाः प्रमाणम्। कर्षकवणिक्पशुपालकुसीदिकारवः स्वे स्वे वर्गे। [II. 2; 20, 21. Ānandāsvama ed.]

[2] तेभ्यो यथाधिकारमर्थान्प्रत्यवहृत्य धर्मव्यवस्था [II. 2. 22. ibid.].

[3] जातिजानपदान्धर्मान् श्रेणीधर्मांश्च धर्मवित्।
समीक्ष्यकुलधर्मांश्च स्वधर्मं प्रतिपादयेत्॥

to the law, that he shall establish as law, if it be not opposed to the laws of countries, families, and castes' [1] [VIII. 46]. This shows that the king was bound to respect the laws of these various local bodies or groups and could not enforce his own law without reference to them—provided such local laws did not run counter to the sacred law. As 'laws of districts' the commentators instance those of the Kuru, Kāpiśa or Kāśmira countries or of the natives of different countries.[2] In the case of a conquered country the victorious king must also, according to Manu, make authoritative the lawful customs of the conquered just as they are stated to be [3] [VII. 203]. The authority of local laws is also affirmed by Āpastamba [4] [II. 15. 1] and Baudhāyana [5] [I. 2. 6]. The opinion of Manu is reiterated by Vasiṣṭha [6] [I. 17]: 'Manu has declared that the laws of countries, castes, and families (may be followed) in

1 सद्भिराचरितं यत्स्यात् धार्मिकैश्च द्विजातिभिः ।
तद्देशकुलजातीनामविरुद्धं प्रकल्पयेत् ॥

2 "कुरु कापिशकाश्मीरादिदेशो नियताम्बधिः" (मेधातिथिः) ।
"यथादाक्षिणात्यानां मातुलसुता परिणयनम्" (नन्दनः), i.e. 'e.g. the marrying of the daughter of the maternal uncle as prevalent among the people of the Dākṣinātya (Deccan).'

3 प्रमाणानिचकुर्वीत तेषां धर्म्यान् यथोदितान् ।

4 एतेन देशकुलधर्मा व्याख्याताः ।

5 तत्र तत्र देशप्रामाण्यमेव स्यात् ।

6 देशधर्म जातिधर्मकुलधर्मान् श्रुत्यभावदब्रवीन्मनुः ।

the absence of (rules of) the revealed texts'. Again [XIX. 7][1]: 'Let the king, paying attention to all the laws of countries, castes, and families make the four castes (*varṇa*) fulfil their particular duties.' In this passage the word *jāti* is explained by one commentator as a tribe, to distinguish it from *varṇa*, meaning class or caste.

But if the king had to respect the laws of the local bodies he had also to see that the members thereof observed their own laws, violations of which he was bound to punish. Thus Yājñavalkya says [I. 361]: 'The king must discipline and establish again on the path (of duty) all such as have erred from their own laws, whether families, castes, guilds, associations, or people of certain districts.'[2] Viṣṇu [III. 2][3] also holds that the duty of the king is to keep the four castes and the four orders in the practice of their respective duties. Nārada also has the same opinion [X. 2]: 'Among heretics, Naijamas, guilds, corporations, troops, or companies of soldiers, assemblages of kinsmen and other associations the king must maintain the usages settled among them,

[1] देशधर्म जातिधर्मकुलधर्मान् सर्वान् वैताननुप्रविश्य राजा चतुरोवर्णान् स्वधर्मे स्थापयेत्।

[2] कुलानिजातीः श्रेणीश्च गणान् जनपदांस्तथा।
स्वधर्मचलितान् राजा विनीय स्थापयेत् पथि॥

[3] प्रजापरिपालनम् वर्णाश्रमणां स्वे स्वे धर्मेव्यवस्थापनम्।

both in the fortified towns and in the open country'.[1] Lastly, Vasiṣṭha also holds that the king is to make the four castes or classes fulfil their respective particular duties [XIX. 7, quoted above].

As a necessary corollary to the above power the king had the authority to enforce by means of adequate penal measures the due respect for guild-laws, guild-compacts, or contracts and agreements entered into by individual members with their associations. Manu [VIII. 221] says: 'A righteous king shall apply this law of fines in villages and and castes (*jāti*) to those who break an agreement'.[2] Again [VIII. 219]. 'If a man belonging to a corporation inhabiting a village or a district, after swearing to an agreement breaks it through avarice, (the king) shall banish him from his realm'.[3] The agreement is thus defined and explained by Bṛhaspati: 'When (the people of a village or province execute a deed of mutual agreement, the purpose of which is not opposed to the interests of the king, and in accordance with sacred law it is designated as

1 पाषण्डि नैगमश्रेणी पूगव्रात गणादिषु ।
संरक्षेत्समयं राजा दुर्गेजनपदेतथा ॥

2 एतद्दण्डविधिं कुर्याद्धार्मिकः पृथिवीपतिः ।
ग्राम जाति समूहेषु समयव्यभिचारिणाम् ॥

3 योग्रामदेशसंघानां कृत्वा सत्येन संविदम् ।
विसंवदेन्नरो लोभात्तंराष्ट्राद्विप्रवासयेत् ॥

a deed of agreement' [VIII. 9].[1] Again: 'A compact formed among villagers, companies of artisans and associations is called an agreement; such an agreement must be observed both in times of distress and for acts of piety' [XVII. 5].[2] Nārada also has the following: 'The aggregate of rules settled among heretics, followers of the Veda, Naigamas, and others is called *samaya* (compact or established usage)' [X. 1].[3] It would thus appear that the agreement herein defined refers to the fundamental agreement on which the association rests, the basis or constitution of the guild, rather than to temporary and minor contracts, the deliberate transgression of the compact being visited accordingly with the exemplary punishment of banishment. Thus Viṣṇu says: 'He who violates their established rule shall also be banished' [V. 168].[4] Yājñavalkya expressly lays it down as the duty of the king to keep the guilds to their constitutional pacts [II. 192].[5] Nārada likewise imposes upon the

1 ग्रामो देशश्च यत्कुर्य्यात् सत्यलेख्यम्परस्परम् ।
राजाविरोधिधर्म्मार्थं संवित् पत्रं वदन्ति तत् ॥

2 ग्रामश्रेणिगणानाञ्च सङ्केतः समयक्रिया ।
बाधाकालेतुसाकार्य्या धर्म्मकार्य्ये तथै च ॥

3 पाषण्डिनैगमादीनांस्थितिः समयउच्यते ।

4 तत् संविदं यश्च लंघयेत् ।

5 भेदंश्चैषां नृपोरक्षेत् पुर्ववृत्तिञ्च पालयेत् ।

king the duty of having the constitution followed by the various public bodies.

But banishment or deportation was the punishment, not only for the violation of the constitution of a corporation, but also for the embezzlement of its public funds. Viṣṇu says: 'He who embezzles goods belonging to a corporation shall be banished' [V. 167].[1] Yājñavalkya is more severe in his punishment of embezzlement, for he adds confiscation of property to banishment [II. 187].[2] Bṛhaspati, however, like Viṣṇu, confines the punishment to deportation of those who injure the joint-stock or general interests of the corporation or violate its constitution in other ways.[3] Lastly, a man, borrowing money for the purposes of his corporation but misappropriating it for his personal purposes, was compelled to refund to the corporation the amount thus borrowed [Kātyāyana].[4]

Certain South Indian inscriptions throw further light on the relations between the king and the local bodies and record several interesting cases of the royal power being invoked and exercised in the

[1] गणद्रव्यापहर्ता विवास्यः ।

[2] गणद्रव्यं हरेद्यस्तु संविदं लंघयेच्चयः ।
सर्वस्वहरणं कृत्वातं राष्ट्राद्विप्रवासयेत् ॥

[3] यस्तुसाधारणं हिंस्यात् . . स निर्वास्यस्ततः पुरादिति ।

[4] गणमुद्दिश्य यत्किञ्चित् कृत्वभक्षितं भवेत् ।
आत्मार्थं विनियुक्तंवा देयं तैरेवतद्भवेत् ॥

interest either of the assemblies or of aggrieved parties. A village assembly had misappropriated some money which was deposited with them as trust-fund for a temple. The temple authorities thereupon sought redress at the hands of the king. He sent for both the parties and instituted a proper inquiry, as a result of which the guilt of the assembly was proved and they were fined and made to refund the money to the temple [*Madras Epigraphy, Annual Report*, 1906–7, p. 71]. An inscription assigned to about A.D. 1291 records the case of the misconduct of a Brahman member of an assembly who brought 'a widow from a foreign country' and lived with her, and against him the assembly reports to the king [ibid., 1908–9, p. 83]. In another inscription the same village assembly for the purpose of paying their homage to the king alienated some land to raise money for the cost of the journey [ibid., p. 84]. An inscription assigned to A.D. 1303 records the case of a village assembly seeking the protection of the king against an intruder into the village who succeeded in intimidating the assembly and confining the members in the temple [ibid.]. Another inscription mentions a village assembly appropriating some of its revenues towards securing the friendship of the king's agents [ibid., 1912–13, p. 114]. In another, money is raised by the assembly for the performance of public prayers on behalf of a sick member of the royal family [ibid., 1898–9, p. 20]. An inscription in the Great Temple of Tanjore [no. 57 in Hultzsch, *S. Ind. Inscr.*, vol. II, p. 227] gives a list of village assemblies each of which was required by the king to supply watchmen for the temple. One of the Tiruvallam inscriptions, assigned to A.D. 991, records the visit of a royal personage to the temple. Observing that the offerings in the temple had been reduced to a minimum and that the temple lamps were only feebly burning, he calls upon the assembly in charge of the trust funds deposited with them for those purposes to render accounts [Hultzsch, *S. Ind. Inscr.*, vol. III, no. 49, p. 102]. Another inscription of the same series [ibid., no. 57] records how two royal officers (the magistrate (*adhikārin*) and the *senāpati*) met at Kāñchipuram and called for the accounts of the villages belonging to the Tiruvallam temple. One of the two decided that the revenues from certain villages (named in the record) should be assigned to the temple for expenses not previously provided for, and called in the aid of a large assembly to make allotments from this revenue for various heads of the temple expenditure. In another [ibid., no. 77] we find a royal officer (*adhikārin*) being delegated to attend the meeting of the assembly, and the clerk of the assembly, writing down the proceedings of the meeting (which was attended by all members 'without a vacancy') in the presence of the officer who was 'walking about'. A most important and typical case of royal interference is recorded in two inscriptions at Uttaramallūr [*Arch. Surv. of India, Annual Report*, 1904–5, p. 134], probably a Brāhmaṇa village, where local government was very near being wrecked by gross mismanagement, giving dishonest men opportunity even to embezzle communal funds and decline to render accounts. The king in A.D. 918–19 deputed one of his Śūdra officers with special instructions to set matters right. The settlement he made not having worked well, the king had again to interfere in A.D. 920–21 and to depute a Brāhmaṇa officer from the Chola country to improve upon the system devised by the Śūdra commissioner more than a year earlier.

Nārada has a general statement which covers the above and other conceivable cases of royal interference in the administration of the local bodies. According to him the ground for that interference arises when those bodies form combinations prejudicial to the interests of the community, or arm themselves without sufficient cause, or quarrel with one another, or take steps which imply hostility to the king, or cause waste of public money, or commit actions morally reprehensible, or contrary to the dictates of religion as laid down in the Vedas or, lastly, when actuated by hatred, the members combine against and boycott one of them.[1]

Treason against the king is dealt with very severely in the South Indian inscriptions. An inscription assigned to A. D. 1230 records the compulsory sale by public auction of lands belonging to certain declared enemies of the state who were members of the village assembly; the price of the lands being fixed by eight Crown officers [*Madras Epigraphy*, *Annual Report*, 1910–11, p. 75]. In another inscription [No. 125 B, ibid., 1912–13, p. 110] the king selects a Vāndya chief as the headman of a village where a disturbance had been created by certain traitors to the king (*rājadrohin*), whom the new chief apparently expelled from the village.

§ 2

ADMINISTRATIVE MACHINERY

With regard to the actual administrative machinery evolved or adopted by these local bodies we have to depend upon the evidence of the later *Smṛtis*

[1] मिथः सङ्घातकरणं अहितौ शस्त्रधारणं।
परस्परोपघातञ्च तेषां राजा न मर्षयेत् ॥
प्रतिकूलञ्च यत् राज्ञः प्रकृत्यवमतञ्च यत्।
बाधकञ्च यदर्थानां तत्तेभ्यो विनिवर्त्तयेत् ॥
दोषवत् करणं यत् स्यात् अनाम्नायप्रकल्पितम्।
प्रवृत्तमपि तत् राजा श्रेयस्कामो निवर्त्तयेत् ॥

such as those of Bṛhaspati, Nārada, and Yājñavalkya. According to Bṛhaspati they are to be governed by a board of from two to five persons selected from the best men of the community. Says he: 'Honest persons, acquainted with the Vedas and with duty, able, self-controlled, sprung from noble families, and skilled in every business, shall be appointed as heads (of an association)' [XVII. 9].[1] Again, 'Two, three, or five persons shall be appointed to look after the welfare of the association' [XVII. 10].[2] These executive officers were called *Samūha-hita-vādinaḥ* and *Kāryya-chintakāḥ*. According to Yājñavalkya these governors should be well-grounded in religion (as embodied in the *Śrutis* and *Smṛtis*), pure in body and mind, and free from avarice [II. 191].[3] They were entitled to the obedience of the members of the corporation. The king was required to enforce their authority by penalty, and the disobedient member was fined by the first amercement. But their authority thus binding on the assembly was also respected by the king himself. As Bṛhaspati states, 'Whatever is done by those (heads of an association) . . . must be approved by

[1] शुचयो वेदधर्म्मज्ञाः दक्षा दान्ताः कुलोद्भवाः ।
सर्व कार्य्यप्रवणाश्च कर्त्तव्याश्च महोत्तमाः ॥

[2] द्वौ त्रयः पञ्च वा कार्य्याः समूहहितवादिनः ।

[3] धर्म्मज्ञाः शुचयोऽलुब्धा भवेयुः कार्यचिन्तकाः ।
कर्तव्यं वचनं तेषां समूहहितवादिनाम् ॥

the king as well, for they are declared to be the appointed managers (of affairs)' [XVII. 18].[1] This is certainly an advance upon the earlier law on the subject. In the case of disputes, however, between these heads and their associations it is ruled that the king shall act as the umpire between them and bring them back to their duty [XVII. 20].[2] Lastly, the heads of associations themselves were also authorized to mete out punishment to all offenders in the guild, whom they could censure, reprimand, and ultimately forsake [XVII. 17].[3] It should also be noted that as the appointment of these officers vested with the public bodies, so also did the power of punishing them. Their decisions regarding the same were formally notified to the king who enforced them, if they could not.

Sir Henry Maine stated that 'in the almost inconceivable case of disobedience to the award of the village council the sole punishment or the sole certain punishment would appear to be universal disapprobation' [*Village Communities in the East and West*, p. 68]. But we have seen from the

1 तैः कृतं यत्स्वधर्म्मेण निग्रहानुग्रहं नृणाम् ।
तद्राज्ञाप्यनुमन्तव्यं निसृष्टार्था हि ते स्मृताः ॥

2 मुख्यैः सह समूहानां विसंवादो यदा भवेत् ।
तदा विचारयेद्राजा स्वधर्म्मे स्थापयेच्च तान् ॥

3 कुलश्रेणीगणाध्यक्षाः पुरदुर्गनिवासिनः ।
वाग्धिग्दमं परित्यागं प्रकुर्य्युः पापकर्म्मिणाम् ॥

above evidence that the authority of the local bodies was maintained ultimately not merely by the moral sanction of the public opinion of the community, but was also enforced by the legal sanction of punishment inflicted by the king. This is clear from the evidence of certain South Indian inscriptions, in one of which of about A.D. 1230 a village assembly decides that any one going against the interests of the village 'should suffer as the *grāma-drohins* do' [*Madras Epigraphy, Annual Report*, 1910–11, p. 75]. This means that injuring the interests of the community is treated as treason against the commonweal and punishable like treason against the king (*rāja-drohin*). The same significance is borne by the term *grāmā-kaṇṭaka* ('a village pest') in the Uttaramallūr inscription [*Arch. Surv. of India*, 1904–5, p. 144].

As regards the composition of these administrative boards we have some interesting evidence in some of the *Smṛtis*. Thus Manu states: 'Whatever an assembly, consisting either of at least ten, or of at least three persons who follow their prescribed occupations, declares to be law, the legal (force of) that one must not dispute' [XII. 110].[1] Again: 'Three persons who each know one of the

[1] दशावरा वा परिषद्यं धर्मं परिकल्पयेत्।
त्र्यवरावापि वृत्तस्था तं धर्मं न विचालयेत्॥

three principal Vedas, a logician, a Mīmāṁsaka, one who knows the Nirukta, one who recites (the Institutes of) the sacred law, and three men belonging to the first three orders shall constitute an assembly consisting of at least ten members' [XII. 111].[1] Gautama also makes the same statement: 'They declare that an assembly (*pariṣad*, shall consist) at least (of) the ten following (members, viz.) four men who have completely studied the four Vedas, three men belonging to the (three) orders enumerated first, (and) three men who know (three) different (Institutes) of law' [XXVIII. 49].[2] Similarly, Baudhāyana: 'Four men who each know one of the four Vedas, a Mīmāṁsaka, one who knows the Aṅgas, one who recites (the works on) the sacred law, and three Brāhmaṇas belonging to three different orders constitute an assembly consisting of at least ten members' [I. 1. 1. 8].[3] The three different orders in the above passages mean those of the student, the householder, and the hermit, or according to some commentators, the ascetic, because hermits (*Vānaprasthas*) cannot serve as members of *pariṣads*,

[1] त्रैविद्योहैतुकस्तर्की नैरुक्तोधर्मपाठकः ।
त्रयश्चाश्रमिणः पूर्वे परिषत्स्याद्दशावरा ॥

[2] चत्वारश्चतुर्णां पारगा वेदानां प्रागुत्तमा त्रय आश्रमिणः पृथग्धर्मविदस्त्रय एतान्दशावरान्परिषदित्याचक्षते ॥

[3] चातुर्वैद्यं विकल्पीच अंकविद्धर्मपाठकः ।
आश्रमस्थाः त्रयो विप्रा पर्षदेषा दशावरा ॥

as they live in the forest, while professed students are included because 'they are declared to be particularly holy in the *Dharmaskandha-brāhmaṇa*' [Bühler, *S.B.E.*, vol. XIV, p. 144 n.]. Secondly, it is to be noted that all the three twice-born castes, the Brāhmaṇas, Kṣatriyas and Vaiśyas, were represented on these assemblies, but the representatives must be such as 'follow the prescribed occupations' for the caste they belong to, as laid down by Manu. It would, therefore, be a mistake to suppose that the Hindu law-givers made the assemblies exclusively Brāhmaṇa in their composition. If there is any doubt on the point the following passages from Āpastamba will serve to clear it. He says: 'It is difficult to learn the sacred law from (the letter of) the Vedas only): but by following the indications it is easily accomplished. The indications for these are: 'He shall regulate his course of action according to the conduct which is unanimously recognized in all countries by men of the three twice-born castes who have been properly obedient (to their teachers), who are aged, of subdued senses, neither given to avarice nor hypocrites' [II. 11. 29.[1] 13–14]. Thirdly,

[1] दुष्करा धर्मसमाप्तिस्समाम्नानेन । लक्षणकर्मणात्तु समाप्यते । तत्रलक्षणम् । सर्वजनपदेष्वेकान्त समाहितमार्याणां वृत्तं सम्यग्विनीतानां वृद्धानामात्मवतामलोलुपानामदाम्भिकानां वृत्त सादृश्यं भजेत । एवमुभौलोकावभिजयति ॥

the number of the assembly varies from ten to three according to Manu [XII. 110 and 112].[1]

The evidence of the *Smṛtis* is confirmed by that of some inscriptions in South India. These mention assemblies which appear to have consisted of 'all the residents of a village including cultivators, professionals, and merchants' [*Madras Epigraphic Report*, 1912–13, p. 98].

Some of the *Smṛtis* refer to assemblies of Brahmans, but these were created by the king [*Rājakṛta*] and not by the public bodies (*Samūhakṛta*). It was the practice of the king in early times to establish in every city with gifts of free quarters and rent-free lands, a body of learned Brahmans with a prescribed course of duties, mainly religious.[2] The Brahman assembly thus constituted had primarily to attend to the moral and spiritual welfare of the people, besides observing their own

[1] दशावरावा परिषद्वं धर्मं परिकल्पयेत् ।
त्र्यवरावापि वृत्तस्था तं धर्मं न विचालयेत् ॥
ऋग्वेदविद्यजुर्विच्च सामवेदविदेव च । त्र्यवरा परिषज्ज्ञेया धर्मसंशयनिर्णये ॥

[2] राजा कृत्य पुरे स्थानं ब्राह्मणान्न्यस्य तत्र तु ।
त्रैविद्यान् वृत्तिमत् ब्रूयात् स्वधर्म्मः पाल्यतामिति ॥
[Yājñavalkya]

वेदविद्याविदो विप्रान् श्रोत्रियानग्निहोत्रिणः ।
संस्कृत्य स्थापयेत् तत्र तेषां वृत्तिं प्रकल्पयेत् ॥
अनाच्छेद्यकरास्तेषां प्रदद्यात् गृहभूमय ।
भुक्तभाव्याश्च नृपतिर्लेखयित्वा स्वशासने ॥—[Bṛhaspati]

duties [*Svadharmapālyatām*] to assist them in the discharge of their daily, occasional, and optional religious duties, to officiate in ceremonies undertaken with a view to averting providential visitations and ensuring public peace and prosperity; and in giving authoritative decisions on doubtful points.[1] But the assembly was also entrusted with certain other secular duties embracing some of the important interests of communal life, such as protection of grazing grounds and water courses, looking after temples and places of public worship and the like. A passage in the *Vīramitrodaya* adds the further duty of feeding people found in a helpless condition in the city, and of preventing the export to foreign countries of such goods as may endanger the interests of the community.[2]

The Sabhās or assemblies of the South Indian inscriptions were also generally to be found in *Brahmadeya* (that is, Brahman) villages and were almost entirely constituted by Brahmans. The

[1] नित्यं नैमित्तकं काम्यं शान्तिकं पौष्टिकं तथा।
पौराणां कर्म्म कुर्य्युस्ते सन्दिग्धेऽर्थे च निर्णयम् ॥—[Bṛhaspati]

[2] निजधर्म्माविरोधेन यस्तु सामयिको भवेत्।
सोऽपि यत्नेन संरक्ष्या धर्म्मो राजकृतश्च य ॥

[Yājñavalkya]

The *Vīramitrodaya* thus explains: "गोप्रचारोदकरक्षणदेवगृहपालनादिरूपः" And again: "यावत् पथिकं भोजनं देयं अस्मद्‌राष्ट्रमण्डले तुरगादयो न स्थापनीयाः इत्येवं रूपः ॥"

rules laid down in the famous Uttaramallūr inscriptions of the time of Parāntaka I [*Arch. Surv. of India*, 1904–5, pp. 131–45] for membership on village committees—rules to which we shall refer below—appear to apply purely to such Brahmanical Sabhās.

The recently published *Madras Epigraphy Report* for 1918 brings to light a very valuable and interesting piece of evidence regarding the philanthropic activities of the village administrations of ancient India in the south. It is an inscription (no. 333 of 1917) of the time of Rājendra-Chola I, not earlier than A. D. 1023. It records the endowment, by the assembly of the village named Rājarāja-chaturvedi maṅgalam, of certain charities in connexion with a temple with the object of securing success to the arms of that Chola 'Napoleon' through the grace of the deity. The charities were mainly intended for maintaining a college for Vedic study and also an attached hostel for students. Arrangements were made for feeding students as described below:

(*a*) 75 studying the Ṛgveda;
(*b*) 75 studying the Yajurveda;
(*c*) 20 studying the Chhāndoga-Sāma;
(*d*) 20 studying the Talavakāra-Sāma;
(*e*) 20 studying the Vājasaneya;
(*f*) 10 studying the Atharva;

(*g*) 10 studying the Baudhāyanīya Gṛha-kalpa and Gaṇa;

(*h*) 40 learning the *Rūpāvatāra*;

(*i*) 25 learning the Vyākaraṇa;

(*j*) 35 learning the Vrabhākara;

(*k*) 10 learning the Vedānta.

340

Thus the total number of students of this Sanskrit college who went into residence comes up to 340. The tutorial staff of the college included, among others, the following ten professors of the Vedas:

(*a*) 3 for the Ṛgveda;

(*b*) 3 for the Yajus;

(*c*) 1 for the Chhāndoga-Sāma;

(*d*) 1 for the Talavakāra-Sāma;

(*e*) 1 for the Vājasaneya;

(*f*) 1 for the Baudhāyanīya Gṛha, Kalpa, and Kāṭhaka.

It is interesting to note that the teachers in some of the subjects were paid for their instruction according to what economists know as the 'piece-work' system. Thus the professor of Vyākaraṇa was paid one *kalañju* of gold per *adhyāya* taught.

No. 343 of 1917 refers to the hostel attached to the temple where provision was made for feeding no less than 506 Brahmans, among whom were the Brahmans versed in the Vedas, Brahmans in general, and the Srī-Vaiṣṇavas. This number probably included the 340 students of the Sanskrit college mentioned above. It is also stated in the record that 'the great men in charge of the *ūrvāriyam* (i.e. the village supervision committee) were made responsible for the daily supply of the firewood required for the hostel. It is further stated that Brahman merchants were lent some money by the assembly, the interest on which was paid by them in kind, in the shape of supplying sugar and other necessaries; and half the surplus quantity of ghee, milk, and curds left after meeting the requirements of worship was made over to the hostel.

Examples of these benefactions help to modify the impression that religious charities in India have always flowed in one particular channel and assumed one stereotyped form, viz. the direct furtherance of the worship of the gods. The type of charities we have just considered shows conclusively how the religious sense of the people in these ancient times was quite sound and even 'modern' in its tendencies, by endowing not simply the temples of gods, but also the hardly less sacred temples of learning, with institutions aiming at the relief of human suffering, thereby recognizing that the service of man was not the least important mode of serving and worshipping God.

CHAPTER V

ADMINISTRATION OF JUSTICE

ONE of the most important functions of the local bodies was, of course, the administration of justice. According to Bṛhaspati 'Judicial assemblies are of four sorts: stationary, not stationary, furnished with the king's signet ring, and directed by the king. A stationary court meets in a town or village; one not stationary is called movable; one furnished with the king's signet-ring is superintended by the chief judge; one directed by the king is held in the king's presence' [I. 2–3].[1] The relations between these different kinds of courts of justice are thus indicated by Nārada: 'Family meetings (*kula*), corporations (*śreṇī*), village assemblies (*gaṇa*), one appointed by the king, and the king himself are invested with the power to decide law-suits; and of these each succeeding is superior to the one preceding it in order'

1 प्रतिष्ठिताप्रतिष्ठिता मुद्रिता शासिता तथा ।
चतुर्विधा सभा प्रोक्ता सभ्याश्चैव तथाविधाः ॥
प्रतिष्ठिता पुरे ग्रामे चला नामाप्रतिष्ठिता ।
मुद्रिताध्यक्षसंयुक्ता राजयुक्ता च शासिता ॥

[I. 7].[1] The significance of this passage from Nārada is thus brought out by the commentator Asahāya: 'A suit decided in a village goes on appeal to the city (court). What has been decided in the city (court) goes (on appeal) before the king (i.e. the king's court); but there is no appeal from the decision of the king, whether right or wrong.'[2] We are not, however, concerned with the higher or king's courts (forming the last two varieties in Bṛhaspati's classification of courts) but only with the lower and local courts (the first two classes of courts mentioned by Bṛhaspati). These lower and local courts were, according to the *Smṛtis*, constituted by the *kula*, the *śreṇī*, the *gaṇa*, or the *pūga*. The gradation of the courts indicated by Nārada is also indicated by other law-givers. Bṛhaspati states: 'Relatives, companies (of artisans), assemblies (of co-habitants) and other persons duly authorized by the king should decide law-suits among men, excepting causes concerning violent crimes (*sāhasa*). Meetings of kindred, companies (of artisans) assemblies (of co-habitants) and chief judges are declared to be resorts for the passing of a sentence to whom he whose cause has been previously tried may appeal

1 कुलानि श्रेणयश्चैव गणाश्चाधिकृतो नृपः ।
प्रतिष्ठा व्यवहाराणां गुर्वेभ्यस्तूत्तरोत्तरम् ॥

2 ग्रामे दृष्टः पुरे याति पुरे दृष्टस्तु राजनि ।
राज्ञा दृष्टः कुदृष्टो वा नास्ति पौनर्भवो विधिः ॥

in succession'. This is further explained thus: 'When a cause has not been (duly) investigated by meetings of kindred it should be decided after due deliberation by companies (of artisans); when it has not been duly examined by companies (of artisans it should be decided) by assemblies (of cohabitants); and when it has not been (sufficiently) made out by such assemblies (it should be tried) by appointed (judges)' [I. 28–30]. Yājñavalkya [II. 30][1] also mentions a similar gradation of local courts such as *kula*, *śreṇī*, and *pūga* arranged in the ascending order of importance, the *kula* being the lowest court composed of kinsmen for arbitration in small matters, from which an appeal lay to the next higher courts. The *śreṇī* has been defined by the *Mitākṣarā*[2] as the court constituted by traders or artisans including men of different castes but pursuing similar means of livelihood, and the *pūga* as the court constituted by men of different castes and occupations but inhabiting the same village or town. It was ruled that if an appeal was lost the appellant must pay double what he was fined by the lower court. The meaning given by the *Mitākṣarā* for the different courts

[1] नृपेणाधिकृताः पूगाः श्रेणयोऽथ कुलानि च।
पूर्वं पूर्वं गुरुज्ञेयं व्यवहारविधौ नृणाम्॥

[2] पूगाः समूहाः भिन्नजातीनां भिन्नवृत्तीनां एकस्थाननिवासिनां यथा ग्रामनगरादयः। श्रेणयो नानाजातीनां एकजातीनामप्येकजातीयकर्म्मोपजीविनां संघाताः॥

makes it clear that their gradation was determined by their numerical strength and the degree in which they represented the various interests, classes or castes in the community concerned. Thus the *pūga* was the highest court because it was numerically the largest assembly, on which were represented not merely the different castes, as in the *śreṇī*, but also the interests of different crafts, trades, or occupations in the village or township.

The principle underlying these lower and local courts has been admirably put by the *Śukranīti*. In cases of dispute the best men of the locality concerned can alone be the proper judges.[1] The application of the principle thus laid down is shown in the following passage: 'Foresters are to be tried with the help of foresters, merchants by merchants, soldiers by soldiers, and in the village by persons who live with both parties' [IV. 5. 24]. This is indeed an echo of the earlier *Smṛti* works. Bṛhaspati says: 'For persons roaming the forest, a court should be held in the forest; for warriors, in the camp; and for merchants in the caravan'. Again: 'Cultivators, artisans (such as carpenters and others), artists, money-lenders, companies (of tradesmen),

[1] अभियुक्तास्त्रयेतच्च यन्निबन्धनियोजनाः ।
तत्तत्यगुणदोषाणां त एव हि विचारकाः ॥
आरण्यास्तु स्वकैः कुर्युः सार्थिकाः सार्थिकैः सह ।
सैनिकाः सैनिकैरेव ग्रामेऽप्युभयवासिभिः ॥

dancers, persons wearing the token of a religious order (such as Pāśupatas) and robbers should adjust their disputes according to the rules of their own profession'. Further: '(the king) should cause the disputes of ascetics and of persons versed in sorcery and witchcraft to be settled by persons familiar with the three Vedas only, and not decide them himself' [I. 25–7].[1] The same principle of neighbourhood and local knowledge is also recognized by Manu when he holds 'the indigenous (inhabitants of the country, be they) Kṣatriyas, Vaiśyas, or Śūdras' as being alone competent to give evidence [VIII. 62].[2] The principle was held to be essential in settling disputes regarding boundaries, on which the following rules are laid down: 'If there be no witnesses let your men who dwell on all the four sides of the two villages make a decision concerning the boundary' [VIII. 258].[3] 'The decision concerning the boundary-marks of fields, wells, tanks, of gardens and houses depends upon (the evidence of) the

1 कीनाशाः कारुकाः शिल्पिकुसीदिश्रेणीनर्तकाः ।
लिंगिनस्तस्कराः कुर्य्युः स्वेनधर्म्मेण निर्णयम् ॥
तपस्विनां तु कार्य्याणि त्रैविद्यैरेव कारयेत् ।
मायायोगविदां चैव न स्वयं कोपकारणात् ॥

2 गृहिणः पुत्त्रिणो मौलाः क्षत्त्रविट्शूद्रयोनयः ।
अर्थ्युक्ताः साक्ष्यमर्हन्ति न ये केचिदनापदि ॥

3 साक्ष्यभावेतु चत्वारोग्रामाः सामन्तवासिनः ।
सीमाविनिर्णयं कुर्युः प्रयताराजसन्निधौ ॥

neighbours'. On failure of the above kinds of witnesses 'the evidence even of the following inhabitants of the forest' was admissible on account of their local knowledge, viz., 'hunters, fowlers, herdsmen, fishermen, root-diggers, snake-catchers, gleaners, and other foresters' [ibid., 259, 260, 262].[1] Yājñavalkya [II. 153–5][2] has also the same regulation: 'In disputes relating to boundaries of land under cultivation persons residing in surrounding villages, aged men and other (competent persons), cow-herds, persons cultivating boundary lands and all persons living on forest produce should determine those boundary (disputes).' Again: 'Or persons from neighbouring villages equal in number (i.e. two or four villagers)—four, eight, or ten—should settle the boundary lines.' Finally, the *Kauṭilīya* will have all disputes regarding the boundary between

1 सामन्तानाम भावे तु मौलानाम् सीम्नि साक्षिणाम् ।
इमानप्यनुयुञ्जीत पुरुषान्वनगोचरान् ॥
व्याधांश्शाकुनिकान्गोपान्कैवर्तान् मूलखानकान् ।
व्यालग्राहानुञ्छवृत्तीनन्यांश्च वनचारिणः ॥
क्षेत्रकूपतडागानामारामस्य गृहस्य च ।
सामन्तप्रत्ययो ज्ञेयः सीमा सेतुविनिर्णयः ॥

2 सीम्नो विवादे क्षेत्रस्य सामन्ताः स्थविरादयः ।
गोपा सीमाकृषाणा ये सर्वे च वनगोचराः ॥
नयेयुरेते सीमानं स्थलांगारतुषद्रुमैः ।
सेतुवल्मीकनिम्नास्थि चैत्याद्यैरुपलक्षिताम् ॥
सामन्तावा समाग्रामा चत्वारोऽष्टौ दशापिवा ।
रक्तस्रग्वसनाः सीमां नयेयुः क्षितिधारिणः ॥

any two villages settled by neighbours or elders of five or ten villages, and disputes arising in the same village by the elders of the neighbourhood or of the village (*grāma-vṛddhāḥ*). It is also stated that all kinds of disputes shall depend for their settlement on the evidence to be furnished by neighbours. We may also cite the opinion of Vasiṣṭha: 'In a dispute about a house or a field reliance (may be placed on the depositions of) neighbours' [XVI. 13].[1] As explained by Kauṭilya the decision of these courts was that of the majority of the persons constituting the court.[2]

The local courts took cognizance of both civil and criminal cases. In the *Kauṭilīya* there occurs a passage in which power seems to be given to the headman of the village to deport out of it criminals like a thief or an adulterer. In some of the South Indian inscriptions there are given interesting details regarding the administration of criminal law. 'A certain individual shot [an arrow at] a man belonging to his own village by mistake. Thereupon the governor and the people of the district to which the village belonged assembled together and decided that the culprit should not die for the offence committed by him through carelessness.' He was not,

[1] गृहक्षेत्रविरोधे सामन्तविरोधेऽपि लेख्यप्रत्ययः।

[2] क्षेत्रविवादं सामन्तग्रामवृद्धाः कुर्युः तेषां द्वधीभावे यतो बहवः शुचयाऽनुमता वा ततो नियच्छेयुः।

however, allowed to escape scot-free, but was made to atone for his action by the penalty of providing for a perpetual sacred lamp at the temple, for which he had to assign sixteen cows to the village assembly. There are two other instances of similar trials connected with shooting accidents or unintentional homicide in which the assembly administered justice without troubling the governor, thus showing how the people 'played a more important part at such trials than even the governor himself'. An inscription of about A.D. 1054 records the suicide of a woman whom a village officer had put through an ordeal for her resistance to certain taxes for which she did not hold herself liable. A meeting of the people from 'the four quarters, eighteen districts and the various countries' was held. The officer was declared guilty and fined. [See *Madras Epigraphy Reports*, 1899–1900, § 26; 1906–7, § 42.]

CHAPTER VI

MUNICIPAL FUNCTIONS

LOCAL bodies in ancient India had also their municipal departments. They are termed *samūhas* for the purpose in some of the *Smṛtis*. For the proper discharge of civic functions and the administration of the various interests of municipal life, an agreement was drawn up in writing forming the Memorandum or Articles of the Association, the members of which were bound to fulfil their legitimate part in promoting the manifold public works necessary for commercial welfare. Deliberate violations of the agreement were severely punished either by banishment or confiscation of property. An attitude of either passive indifference to the agreement, or of opposition to it, was also punished by a heavy fine. Those who created disunion in the association were similarly dealt with. According to the *Kauṭilīya Arthaśāstra*, 'Whoever stays away from any kind of co-operative undertaking, shall send his servants and bullocks to carry on the work, shall have a share in the expenditure but none in the profits' [II. i.].[1] The purposes for the promotion of which these municipal bodies were constituted embraced quite a wide area of useful activity which could not be left to the efforts of individuals, but was proper only for communal enterprise. They are thus enumerated by Bṛhaspati[2]: preservation and maintenance of public halls, temples, tanks, rest-houses, wells for supply of drinking water to travellers, construction of water-courses and places of worship, protection against incursions of wicked people, and relief of the distressed. We thus find that these municipalities addressed themselves, not only to the ordinary material interests of communal life, such as sanitation and water-supply, but also to the interests of public and spiritual life by the provision of halls for public meetings and temples for public worship. They also organized the communal charities which embraced not merely the secular

[1] पुण्यस्थानारामाणां च । सम्भूयसेतुबन्धादप्रकामतः कर्म करबलीवर्दाः कर्म कुर्युः । व्ययकर्मणिच भागी स्यात् । नचांशंलभेत ॥

[2] सभाप्रपादेवगृहतड़ागारामसंस्कृतिः ।
तथानाथदरिद्रानां संस्कारो यजनक्रिया ॥
कुलायनं निरोधश्च कार्यमस्माभिरंशतः ।
यन्नैतल्लिखितं सम्यक् धर्म्म्या सा समयक्रिया ॥

The *Viramitrodaya* thus explains the passage: सभा मण्डपः । प्रपा पानीयशालिका । आरामः उपवनम् । संस्कृतिः जीर्णोद्धारः । संस्कारः उपनयनादिकः प्रेतदहनादिकश्च । यजनक्रिया सोमयागादिकर्त्तृभ्यो दानम् । कुलायननिरोधः कुलायनदुर्भिक्षादि अपगमपर्यन्तस्य धारणम् । There is another reading कुल्यायनविरोधः of which the meaning is कुल्यायाः प्रवर्त्तनप्रतिबन्धौ.

relief of the poor in times of famine and other calamities [*Kulāyana-nirodhaścha*] but also their religious or spiritual ministrations which included the performance of purifying rites for the destitute and poor, viz. arrangements for the cremation of dead paupers, distribution of gifts among people desirous of performing religious acts, &c. Thus the sphere of the administration of Poor Law was widened so as to bring within its compass provision for the spiritual necessities in the life of the destitute as fixed by their *Śāstras*. In another passage Bṛhaspati includes financial support in aid of the idiot, the infirm, the blind, the orphan, the distressed, as also diseased persons and women among the legitimate purposes to which an association could apply its public fund.[1] We should also note that the interests of strangers were not ignored.

Finally, it should be observed that the legitimate activities and functions of the municipalities were not rigidly and strictly restricted within the limits of the agreement aforesaid, but that those bodies were allowed freedom of action against emergencies, provided such action was not contrary to their constitution.[2] [See *Yājñavalkya*.]

1 देयं बालिशवृद्धान्धस्त्रीबालातुररोगिषु।
सन्तातिकादिषु तथा एष धर्म्मः सनातनः॥

2 निज धर्म्माविरोधेन यस्तु सामयिको भवेत्।
सोऽपि यत्नेन संरक्ष्यो धर्म्मो राजकृतश्च यः॥

Much interesting evidence is supplied by South Indian inscriptions as regards one branch of municipal activity, viz. the irrigation works. For this purpose compulsory labour seems to have been employed by the assemblies in the interests of the community.[1] The indigenous irrigation system comprised generally tanks and channels, which were built partly by individual benefactions and partly by communal enterprise. In any case, the duty of maintaining and keeping them in repair came to be recognized by custom as falling upon the village community. Accordingly most of the inscriptions deal with the means employed for repairing them and keeping them in proper condition after they were constructed. The commonest kind of repair which we find mentioned as being necessary was the removal of accumulated silt. Towards this provision was made for the supply of boats, of baskets in which to lift the earth, of labourers, of skilled workmen to take care of the boats, and of fishermen to provide certain kinds of necessaries. As regards actual examples of such works of olden times, we find two tanks in the Chingleput district of the Madras Presidency mentioned in inscriptions of the eighth and ninth centuries A.C. There is

[1] Even the central government sometimes exploited compulsory labour for its own purpose. The great temple of Tanjore, for instance, was built largely by forced labour.

other epigraphic and literary evidence which carries back the existence of irrigation works to still more remote times. An interesting summary of the facts set out in the inscriptions is given by Mr. Venkayya in the *Arch. Surv. Report* for 1903–4. The most famous tank seems to have been Vayiramega-taṭāka at Uttaramallūr in the Chingleput district. An inscription records [ibid., p. 204] the provision in the form of an endowment made by a private individual for removing silt in the tank, which was accepted by the village assembly. Another states that certain ryots, having failed to pay the dues on their holdings, the village assembly paid the amount for them and took over their land for the benefit of the tank for three years. If at the end of that period the defaulters should return and pay up all their dues they were to get back the land, otherwise it would be sold for the benefit of the tank. If any man of Uttaramallūr objected to this course, his land was to be sold similarly and the sale proceeds credited to the tank, while the man himself was to be dealt with as an enemy of the village (*grāma-kaṇṭaka*). If an arbitrator objected he should be banished from the village. There are seven more records which relate to the same tank and express the care of the community for it and the widespread appreciation of its uses. The earliest of them registers a transaction relating apparently to another tank, and imposes on those who violate it a fine to be credited to the funds of the Variyamega tank. The next records a gift of land, and the third a gift of gold accepted by the assembly for the removal of silt during three months of the year. The fourth registers a gift of gold and paddy by a private donor, from the interest of which the assembly had to meet the cost of removing silt for two months. The next two refer to a gift of 200 *kalañju* of gold, the interest from which, amounting to 30 *kalañju* per year, was to be spent annually in removing silt from the tank and depositing it on the bund by the village assembly, who expressed their gratification at this charitable act of the donor, and exempted him from payment of certain taxes. It is interesting to note that the rate of the interest is definitely stated in this record, viz. 15 per cent. per annum, which is higher than the rate usually stated in the inscriptions mentioned above. The last, but not the least interesting, record registers a permanent deposit of 100 *kalañju* of gold with the assembly, from the interest of which they had to provide for the up-keep of a 'second boat' on the tank to be employed in removing silt. Every day a certain specified extent of the tank was to be cleared and the mud deposited on the bund.

A tank with a sluice is mentioned in an inscription in North Arcot district which records a gift of land, the income from which was to be spent in removing silt from a second tank in the same village. Those who look after the gift are assured of acquiring the merit of performing a horse sacrifice! One of the Ukkal inscriptions [Hultzsch, *S. I. Ins.*, vol. III, Part I, p. 9] has the following: 'We, the assembly, shall close (the sluice of) the tank (to collect water for irrigation) and shall cause 500 *kāḍi* of paddy to be supplied as interest every year on these 1000 *kāḍi* of paddy. The great men elected for the year shall cause (the paddy) to be supplied.' The rate of interest in this record is 50 per cent. per annum.

Coming to the times of the Cholas we find stated in an inscription of the twelfth year of the reign of King Parāntaka I (= A. D. 917) that a donation of gold made by one of the king's officers for feeding Brāhmaṇas was utilized by the 'tank supervision committee' to pay the wages of the workmen employed to remove silt in the 'big tank of our village' (named Kāveripāk). The tank must have been built long before A. D. 917.

Most interesting details are given by two inscriptions at Naṅguvaram, assigned roughly to the time of Prince Ariñjaya, son of Parāntaka I, i. e. about the middle of the tenth century A. C. One of them records a sale of land during the reign of the Chola king Rājakesarivarman by the village assembly to a private person on account of the boat plying in the tank. The second furnishes details as to how the income from this land was to be spent. The boat was to be employed for clearing the tank of silt. The operation is fully described—140 baskets of earth, each with capacity to hold 6 *marakkāl* (i. e. about 200 cubic feet) of earth, were to be taken out of the tank and deposited on the bund daily. The establishment comprised a supervisor who received the wages of $1\frac{1}{2}$ *kuruṇi* of paddy *per diem*, and under him 6 labourers who were full-time workmen, and therefore paid higher wages, viz. 1 *padakku* of paddy per head *per diem* for both food and clothing; a carpenter and a blacksmith for repairing the boat, each of whom got annually $2\frac{1}{2}$ *kalam* of paddy; and the fishermen (number not mentioned) who supplied wood for repairs to the boat and got 2 *kalam* of paddy annually. The village assembly had to get the land cultivated and to pay for the whole process out of the income. If they failed to do it, the then reigning king could fine them and get it done (compare other grounds of state-interference with the local bodies given above). Altogether the total annual expenditure for the operation amounted to 412 *kalam* of paddy.[1]

[1] 1 *kalam* = 12 *marakkāl* or *kuruṇi*; 1 *padakku* = 2 *kuruṇi*. Thus the supervisor, carpenter, and blacksmith received less wages than the labourers. Inscriptions of the Chola king Rājarāja I

An inscription of Rājarāja I mentions a 'big tank' at Bāhūr, near Pondicherry, where the villagers agreed to contribute towards the maintenance of the revenue of the tank. The tank committee of the assembly levied the contributions and undertook annual removal of the silt. Any villager refusing to pay had to pay a fine to be credited to the tank-fund under king's orders.. An Ukkal inscription [see p. 137 above] refers to the sale of some land to a private person by the village assembly, who were to provide out of its income for the up-keep of two boats assigned to a tank. The boats were probably meant not only for crossing purposes, as

(A.D. 985–1013) give the rates of wages paid to the various kinds of labourers employed on the temples at Tanjore. '50 *kalam* of paddy was given annually to each drummer and barber; 75 to each under-carpenter and under-accountant; 100 to each of the following, viz. watchmen, dancing girls, washermen, tailors, braziers, and superintending goldsmiths; 150 to a master carpenter; 175 to a lute-player, 200 to the accountant and dancing master. Brāhmaṇa servants got 1 *padakku* of paddy per day, and a *kāśu* annually, while vocalists who had to sing hymns were paid 3 *kuruṇi* per day. Paddy seems to have been sold at the rate of 2 *kalam* per *kāśu*, while the rate of interest was, as we have seen above, 12½ per cent. For 1 *kāśu* 3 sheep could be bought, while 1 she-buffalo was exchanged for 3 cows or 6 ewes; 1200 plantains could be had for 1 *kāśu*.' In another inscription [*S. I. Ins.*, vol. II, Pt. III, p. 259] the wages are indicated in shares of land: thus, a jewel-stitcher got 1½ share, brazier 1 share, master-carpenter 1½ share, superintending goldsmith 1 share, and so forth, and the comparison of these rates with the above will show that 1 share of land probably yielded 100 *kalam* of paddy annually.

explained by Dr. Hultzsch [*S. I. Ins.*, vol. III, p. 15], but also for the usual work of removing the silt.

We need not refer to the irrigation works mentioned in the later Chola, Pāṇḍya, and Vijayanagara inscriptions, but we may notice some in the Telugu and Kanarese countries. These are 'the great tank, a reservoir for the supply of abundant water' built at Tālagunda in the Shimoga district of Mysore by the Kadamba king Kākusthavarman in the first half of the sixth century A. D. [*Ep. Ind.*, vol. VIII, p. 36]; another at Chikballapur in the Kolar district mentioned in a record of A. D. 977–8 [no. 126 of 1892]; and another with a sluice constructed at Sindhuvalli in the Mysore district in A. D. 1106–7 during the reign of the Chola king Kulottuṅga I [no. 3 of 1895]. Several inscriptions at Bāgali in the Bellary district record gifts made to the 'big tank' for repairs, &c.

Some irrigation channels are mentioned in the inscriptions, e. g. the Uyyakkoṇḍān in Trichinopoly district of the time of Rājarāja I, the head-sluice of the Periyavāykkāl in the same district, built of stone during the reign of Rājarāja II, about A. D. 1219.

Remedies against breaches in tank-bunds and other similar accidents beyond human control were generally provided by private charity. Thus in

A. D. 1189–90, for instance, heavy rains caused breaches in the tank at Somaṅgalam (Chingleput), which were repaired by a chief. There were two breaches next year also repaired by him, but he then made a money endowment, from the interest of which the assembly agreed to carry out the instructions of the donor by depositing a certain specified quantity of earth on the bund annually [no. 183 of 1901].

From the evidence adduced above it is clear that tanks, sluices, and irrigation channels were always maintained by local bodies though their construction was often due to private or royal benefactions.[1] The maintenance of tanks chiefly meant the periodical removal of its silt, and the work devolved upon the municipal department—or rather 'the tank committee'—of the village assembly, who were put

[1] The motive for such benefactions was probably connected with the prevailing belief that the spirit of a dead man is consumed by extraordinary thirst, and that it has to be appeased by charities of a water-shed, well, or tank. An instance of this is mentioned in a record of the time of Rājarāja I [see *Mad. Ep. Report*, 1914], and another in the twenty-sixth year of his reign recording a gift of land for maintaining a water-shed in order that the thirsty spirit of his sister, the deceased queen Vīramahādevī (evidently the wife of King Rājendra-Chola I) might be appeased [*Mad. Ep. Report*, 1916, p. 118]. No. 422 of 1915, however, quotes the words of the *Mahābhārata*, stating that the person in whose tank the thirsty cows, beasts, birds, and men drink water obtains the fruit of performing the *Aśvamedha*-sacrifice, thus expressing probably the true motive of these secular charities.

in charge of endowments of both money and land for the purpose by private donors. We have also seen that preservation of tanks was regarded as a religious work, bringing great spiritual merit to the man providing for it. Tanks themselves, like temples, had endowments of land or money of their own, and the repairs were enacted at the expense of these endowments. In the Kanarese country the term *koḍaji* denotes a grant of land rent-free for the purpose of service in connexion with the restoration or construction of tanks or of their maintenance in good order [*Ep. Ind.*, vol. III, p. 51]. In the absence of suitable endowments or private charity the assemblies themselves offered land from the cultivable wastes of the village as an inducement to undertake such works, and where such wastes were not available, nor private enterprise and charity, they themselves undertook them at the joint expense of the villagers, who all benefitted by same. Thus probably arose the custom of *kuḍimarāmat* in Southern India, by which the employment of compulsory labour for repairs to irrigation works is sanctioned.

The manifold kinds of administrative activity shown by these ancient Indian local bodies, embracing not merely the sphere belonging to the ordinary and normal civil functions, but also that covered by much socialistic, philanthropic, and charitable work, undoubtedly imply the existence of an adequate public fund at the disposal of these institutions. We have some evidence on the subject in some of our *Smṛti* works. The sources of the corporation finances are thus indicated by Bṛhaspati [XVII. 24][1]: 'Whatever is obtained or preserved by the members of a fellowship or earmarked for a particular purpose of the society or acquired through the king's favour is common to all (members of the society).' Another source of that joint-stock is indicated by Yājñavalkya [II. 190],[2] viz. the profits which an individual member of the association may earn in the execution of a public work entrusted to him by the association. These profits legally vest in the corporation, and cannot be appropriated by the individual who has reaped them. If he unlawfully appropriates them he has to refund eleven times the amount of the original profits as a penalty. Thus the sources of the public fund of corporations comprise the contributions of individual members, the gifts of the king, the profits earned on public works, and the proceeds from penalties which included confiscation of property for serious offences, as stated by Bṛhaspati and

1 यत्तैः प्राप्तं रक्षितञ्च गणार्थे वा प्रकल्पितम्।
राजप्रसाद लब्धञ्च सर्व्वेषामेव तत्समम्॥

2 सम्हकार्यप्रहितो यल्लभेततदर्पयेत्।
एकादशगुणंदाप्यः यद्यसौ नार्पयेत्स्वयम्॥

Yājñavalkya. But the *Vīramitrodaya* mentions an additional source of municipal revenue, viz. octroi duties on goods sold within municipal limits.[1] The *Vivādaratnākara*, in its chapter on immunities enjoyed by towns, also mentions a few other sources such as those connected with the rights granted to the municipalities to import and export goods without the sanction of government (and thereby earning immunity from the necessary cesses), to levy a duty on goods carried on people's shoulders, and to decide disputes relative to the conduct of the minor associations existing within the municipal limits. When these sources of municipal revenue proved inadequate, recourse was had to private borrowings or state help.[2]

The utilization of this joint-stock was determined by the corporation itself either every month or six months in the manner following,[3] viz. (*a*) by division among the members or partners of the association, or

[1] जनपदेतु क्वचित् विक्रेतृसकाशात् शुल्कग्रहणमित्यनेकविधः समया वर्त्तते।

[2] निष्क्रमणं प्रवेशेष्वनिवेदनम् स्कन्धबाह्येषु शुल्को गणसमयश्रेणीपूगव्यवहारनिष्ठा।

[3] देयं बालिशवृद्धान्ध स्त्रीबालातुररोगिषु।
सन्तानिकादिषु तथा एष धर्म्मः सनातनः॥
ततो लभेत यत्किञ्चित् सर्व्वेषामेव तत्समम्।
षाण्मासिकं मासिकं वा विभक्तव्यं यथांशतः॥
यत्तैः प्राप्तं रक्षितञ्च गणार्थे वा प्रकल्पितम्।
राजप्रसादलब्धञ्च सर्वेषामेव तत्समम्॥—[Bṛhaspati]

(*b*) by donations to the deserving, such as the infirm, diseased, distressed, blind, and idiotic, orphans and helpless women, or (*c*) by expenditure on such public works as might be decided upon by the guild. The division of the net joint-fund among the members was of course proportioned according to the amount contributed to the fund by each individual member (i. e. according to his share in the joint-stock). It is also clear that all funds donated by the king to a single member of a corporation should belong to all or the entire body, thus showing the communistic principles on which the corporation was governed. ['Whatever is acquired through the king's favour is common to all', Bṛhaspati, XVII. 24]. All expenditures of the society, besides royal gifts, are similarly common to all.

CHAPTER VII

CONSTITUTION

According to the evidence of South Indian inscriptions the assemblies were endowed with adequate resources to enable them to perform their various functions properly. They seem to have been the absolute proprietors of the village lands. Lands newly acquired or settled vested in them. They also sanctioned settlements and the taxes for them. They were even authorized by the king to confiscate and sell the land for which no taxes had been paid for two years [no. 620 of 1909 and no. 647 of the same year; on other points see the series of Ukkal inscriptions in Hultzsch, *South Ind. Ins.*, vol. III, pp. 1–18]. Their banking departments, which received deposits connected with charities and benefactions and paid out interest on them, placed at their disposal much money to handle and utilize. One of their main businesses seems to have been land-jobbing. They had often to sell lands for charitable and religious endowments, and received not merely the purchase-money, but also an extra sum from the interest of which they could pay the state dues fixed for the alienated lands which they themselves made tax-free. Thus they were themselves in a position to make their own grants of land for communal purposes and benefactions, of which we have so many instances recorded in the inscriptions.

It has already been made clear that the evidence derived from South Indian inscriptions is far more copious and elaborate than that from the northern. The evidence of the south brings out the fact that the village assemblies of ancient India had developed a considerable differentiation of functions and also different organs for the exercise of each function. As has been already pointed out, it is not quite clear from the northern testimony of both literature and inscriptions how far the same assembly exercised a multiplicity of functions, administrative, judicial, municipal, and the like, or whether there were developed differently constituted and composed bodies to administer the different interests of communal life. So far as the purely judicial functions were concerned, the evidence of the *Smṛtis* set forth above probably points to the growth of independent institutions for the purpose, but no such definite opinion can be pronounced in respect of the other functions. The gaps and deficiencies of the northern evidence are, however, supplied and made good by the southern, which is remarkably rich in details such as enable us to form a clear idea of the structure of the local government, its organs and functions, the character of the administrative machinery devised as a whole, as also of its different parts.

The evidence dates from the ninth century A. C. The group of 'Ukkal inscriptions' first supplies definite details on the subject. The village of Ukkal was governed by an assembly sometimes called *Sabhā* and sometimes *Mahāsabhā*. The *Sabhā* is mentioned for instance in inscriptions nos. 85, 110, 111, 146 and the like in *South Indian Inscriptions*, vol. I. The *Mahāsabhā* is mentioned is no. 42 [ibid.]. The main or central assembly was ṣubdivided into several committees, the total number and designations of which have to be gathered from various inscriptions of different times. An inscription of the Gaṅga-Pallava king Kampavarman (ninth century A. C.), for instance, registers an endowment accepted by the assembly who appoint 'the great men elected for the year' (i. e. of the annual committee) as trustees of the endowment [no. 5, ibid.]. The same committee is referred to in inscription no. 7 and also in nos. 11, 12, 13. No. 14 states: 'The great men who manage the affairs of the village in each year shall supervise this charity', viz. the grant of land by a cultivator named Śenai from the proceeds of which water and fire-pans had to be supplied to a *maṇḍapa* frequented by Brāhmaṇas. The next committee mentioned is that of 'the great men in charge of the tank'. No. 6 in recording the grant of an assembly of a daily supply of rice and oil to a temple states that 'the great men elected for (the supervision of) the tank shall be entitled to levy a fine of (one) *kalañju* of gold in favour of the tank-fund from those betel-leaf sellers in this village who sell (betel-leaves) elsewhere but at the temple of Pidāri.' The tank committee is also mentioned in nos. 11 and 12. No. 13 mentions 'the great *Bhaṭṭas* elected for the tank'. The third committee mentioned is that formed by those in charge of the gardens in no. 12. The Ukkal inscriptions also show that the transactions of the assembly were put in writing by an officer who had the title 'arbitrator', *madhyastha*, mentioned in nos. 2, 3, 6, 10, and 12, and who is once called 'an accountant', *Karaṇattān* [no. 10].

'The Committee of the Assembly' is referred to in an inscription at Ambāsamudram of Varaguṇa-Mahārāja, who reigned probably at the beginning of the ninth century A.C. [*Ep. Ind.*, vol. IX, p. 86]. The committees called *pañchavārī* and *vāragoṣṭhi* (i.e. committee-assembly) are mentioned in an Eastern Chalukya copper-plate grant of the first half of the tenth century A.C., which speaks of 'youths eloquent at committee-assemblies, honoured by the chief people who have made them serve on the committee of five' [*Ep. Ind.*, vol. V, p. 138].

But the most considerable clear light on the system of rural administration in ancient times is thrown by the two famous inscriptions in the Vaikuṇṭha-Perumāl temple at Uttaramallūr, assigned to the tenth century A. C. In the first place, they speak of a number of committees, to each of which they apply a different designation to indicate roughly the sphere of work allotted to it. Secondly, they indicate the method of selection of committee members. Thirdly, they lay down the qualifications determining the eligibility for selection as a committee member. Fourthly, they enumerate the classes of disqualified persons. Fifthly, they lay down the conditions for the appointment of the accountants.

The number and names of the various committees are thus given:

(1) *Annual Committee* (*samvatsara-vāriyam*): this seems to have been the most important, influential, and dignified of all the committees. This is evident from the fact that the election of this committee precedes that of all other committees, and also from the characterization of its personnel. Only 'those who had (previously) been on the "garden committee" and on the "tank committee", those who are advanced in learning, and those who are advanced in age shall be chosen for the "annual committee".'

Thus the annual committee was constituted by the cream of the community, men of ripe old age, mature wisdom, experience in administration, and possessing culture and learning. The number of the committee was fixed at twelve. The committee is also called the committee of annual supervision (*samvatsara-grāma kāryam*) in nos. 466 and 467 of 1912 [*Mad. Ep. Report*, 1913], a designation which points to its superior status among the other committees.

(2) *Garden Committee*: the number of this committee was likewise fixed at twelve.

(3) *Tank Committee*: the number of members was six. The duties of this committee are apparent from the name. They are indicated in detail in numerous inscriptions, some of which have been already cited. The committee were entrusted by the general assembly with all endowments made in favour of tanks in the shape of grants of land, and they had to invest money endowments in the best possible way [see *infra*, p. 197–9]. They utilized the deposits of money in reclaiming waste lands and cultivating it in order to pay out of the produce the interest on the deposit. They had also apparently to look after the cultivation of lands granted to tanks. The income from both these sources was applied to meet the expenses of the annual or occasional operation of the removal of

the silt of tanks and of other necessary repairs to breaches of bunds and to boats employed on the tanks. They had to levy the fines which were to be credited to the tank-fund. Endowments for water-sheds to supply drinking water to thirsty wayfarers were apparently entrusted to them [see no. 75 of 1898].

(4) *Gold Committee*: the number of members was fixed at six. This committee probably regulated the currency.

(5) *Pañcha-vāra Committee*: the number of this also was six. The following note of Venkayya (with slight verbal changes) will explain its character and function: 'Professor Kielhorn translates *pañcha-vāra* by "committee of five" [*Ep. Ind.*, vol. V, p. 138, note 7]. But, as the number of members of this committee is fixed at six, this translation cannot be accepted. Perhaps it supervised the five committees (*pañcha-vāra*) of the village. It is possible that originally there were only five committees in a village, and that the work of these was supervised by the *pañcha-vāra* committee. In the Telugu country it appears to have been a special honour to be placed on this committee, and this honour was probably due to its supervising the work of the other committees. Later on, the number of village committees seems to have been increased, and there appear to have been more than

five committees. Even after this alteration the original name *pañcha-vāra-vāriyam*, given to the supervising committee, probably was retained unaltered' [*Arch. Surv. Report*, 1904–5, p. 145].

The above interpretation of Mr. Venkayya may need to be reconsidered in the light of inscription no. 131 of *Madras Epigraphy Report* for 1912–13, which includes the *pañcha-vāra* among various kinds of taxes or dues payable on land by the tenants who cultivated them, so that *pañcha-vāra-vāriyam* may have been the committee appointed to collect the *pañcha-vāra* dues of the village payable in kind.

(6) *Committee for supervision of justice*: the duty of this committee seems to have been, as its name indicates, to 'supervise the justice' or fairness of the annual elections of the various committees. The inscription (Uttaramallūr, B. in *Ann. Rep. A. S., India*, 1904–5, p. 144) states: 'For appointing the committees after these have retired the members of the "committee for supervision of justice" in the twelve streets (of Uttaramallūr) shall convene an assembly (*kuri*) with the help of the arbitrator.' Thus this committee convened the annual meeting of the assembly and conducted the elections of the various committees whenever they were necessitated by vacancies caused in them by removal of members 'found guilty of offence'.

Next, as to the method of selection of members for the various committees. The village with its twelve streets was divided for purposes of the selection into thirty wards or electoral units. There was a meeting of each ward at which the residents were to assemble, and each of them was required to write down on a ticket the name of the person he voted for after consideration of his eligibility for membership of the committee as defined by the regulations framed by the assembly. The tickets were then to be arranged in separate packets corresponding to the thirty wards. Each packet bore the name of the ward it represented on its 'covering ticket'. The packets were put into a pot. Then the pot was placed before 'a full meeting of the great assembly, including the young and old (members), as also all the temple priests who happened to be in the village on the day "without any exception whatever" in the inner hall (where) the great assembly (meets).' 'In the midst of the temple priests, one of them who happens to be the eldest shall stand up and lift that pot, looking upwards so as to be seen by all people.' One of the young boys who did not know what was inside was then called to pick out one of the packets. The tickets in this packet were then 'transferred to another (empty) pot and shaken', i. e. shuffled thoroughly. The boy then drew one ticket out of the pot and made it over to the arbitrator (*madhyastha*). 'While taking charge of the ticket thus given (to him), the arbitrator shall receive it on the palm of his hand with the five fingers open. He shall read out (the name on) the ticket thus received. The ticket read (by him) shall also be read out by all the priests present in the inner hall. The name thus read out shall be put down (and accepted).' Thirty names were thus to be chosen, representing each of the wards.

It will appear from the above description of the procedure of the election that the people of the whole village regarded themselves at vitally interested in its purity and success, on which depended so largely their common welfare. The weak point in the system, however, was that the method of selection was simply the mechanical one of casting lots instead of voting by ballot, and the consequent process of elimination of names according to the number of votes secured by each. There was universal suffrage, but the democratic principle was not followed up in its complete consequence. Probably the conformity to the conditions of eligibility for membership produced for all practical purposes approximate uniformity of competence and capacity in the persons named on the voting papers or tickets, so that there was not much to choose between them. On the other hand, the method of casting lots would give no scope to canvassing and other electioneering methods of doubtful utility and ethical value. The conditions of eligibility were a sufficient safeguard against the return of a really undesirable person, and the necessary eliminations they involved would leave to chance but very little likelihood of producing any undesirable result. It is significant that the priesthood occupied a dignified position in the meeting of the general assembly, and that their oldest member was chosen as the president of the meeting. The part given to the young is also interesting. The union of God-fearing age with unsophisticated youth must have been naturally productive of the happiest results and preventive of all foul play.

The inscription goes on to say: 'Of the thirty men thus chosen those who had (previously) been on the garden committee and on the tank committee, those who are advanced in learning, and those who are advanced in age shall be chosen for the annual committee. Of the rest, twelve shall be taken for the garden committee, and the remaining six shall form the tank committee. These (last) two committees shall be chosen by "showing the *karai*" (i. e. apparently oral expression of opinion or "selection by acclamation",' as is done even in modern meetings when there is no ground for any special objection to the names suggested). The tenure of office of these elected members of the three committees was 'for full 360 days', after which they had to retire.

For elections to the *pañcha-vāra* and gold committees a similar process was gone through for the selection of thirty names for each of the wards. 'From these thirty twelve men shall be elected. Six out of twelve thus chosen shall form the gold committee, and the remaining six the *pañcha-vāra* committee.' Since the selection by drawing lots of only twelve men out of thirty would inevitably result in the elimination of eighteen wards from representation on those important committees, it was enacted that in future elections 'the wards which have been already represented on these committees shall be excluded and the selection made from the remaining wards by "drawing the *karai*".'

Thirdly, as to the qualifications for membership. The following qualifications are to be possessed by a member to be eligible for nomination by his ward, viz.

(1) He must own more than a quarter (*veli*) of tax-paying land. [*Veli* = 5 acres (Winslow).]

(2) He must live in a house built on his own site.

(3) His age must be below 70 and above 35.

(4) He must know the *Mantra-Brāhmaṇa*, i.e. he must know (the Veda) 'by teaching'; or, according to Venkayya, 'both the *Mantras* and the *Brāhmaṇas*'.

(5) If he owns only one-eighth of land, he must

be proficient in one Veda and one of the four *bhāṣyas* by explaining (it to others).

(6) He must be conversant with business.

(7) He must be virtuous, and his earnings must be honest.

(8) He must not have been on any of the committees for three previous years. This rule, as has been already stated, does not apply to the election to the annual committee, for which the previous membership of the garden and tank committees with the necessary administrative experience it implied, was regarded as a qualifying requisite.

Fourthly, as regards disqualified persons. These comprised the following descriptions of persons:

(*a*) Defaulting committee members (i.e. those who have not submitted accounts) and their relations, however remote, who are thus specified, viz. (1) the sons of the younger and elder sisters of his mother; (2) the sons of his paternal aunt and maternal uncle; (3) the uterine brother of his mother; (4) the uterine brother of his father; (5) his uterine brother; (6) his father-in-law; (7) the uterine brother of his wife; (8) the husband of his uterine sister; (9) the sons of his uterine sister; (10) the son-in-law who has married his daughter; (11) his father; (12) his son.

(*b*) Incorrigible sinners and their relations, however remote. These sinners comprise those against whom are recorded 'the first four of the five great sins', viz. (1) killing a Brāhmaṇa; (2) drinking intoxicating liquors; (3) theft; (4) adultery with the wife of one's spiritual teacher: and (5) associating with any one guilty of these crimes [Manu, XI. 55]. The relations comprise those enumerated above.

(*c*) Outcasts until they perform the necessary expiatory ceremonies, provided the cause of the outcasting being only association with low people, and not any serious moral lapse.

(*d*) Those who are mentally or morally disqualified.

(*e*) Those who are themselves disqualified but do not transmit their disqualification to their relatives. This class includes those who have (1) taken forbidden dishes of any kind [which is equivalent to drinking intoxicating liquor according to Manu (XI. 57)]; (2) committed sins [notably those specified in (*b*) above]; (3) become village pests; and (4) committed incest; and even though they may, by the proper performance of the necessary expiatory ceremonies, prevent the transmission of their own disabilities to their relatives, they will themselves remain disqualified. Expiatory ceremonies might remove religious but not civic and political disabilities of persons guilty of grave offences, social, political, and moral.

With regard to the *pañcha-vāra* and gold committees, which perhaps were not annually appointed, two additional disqualifying circumstances are introduced, viz. (*a*) riding on an ass [which was apparently a punishment for some offence, and hence implied a conviction disqualifying the candidate; Manu (XI. 202) holds driving in a wagon drawn by an ass as a sin]; (*b*) committing forgery, which was no doubt specially disqualifying in regard to membership of a currency committee.

In the above description of the qualifications for membership the age restriction, the educational and property qualifications laid down and the principle of membership by rotation are noteworthy items acceptable even to modern administrators.

We have now considered the evidence of two important groups of epigraphic records which give details about the number, composition, and constitution of the various committees through which the assembly administered local affairs. But it should be noted that the number of committees of such village assemblies does not seem to have been the same everywhere. The number seems to have varied with local conditions. Thus inscriptions found at Tiruppārkadal, near Kāveripāk in the North Arcot district furnish the names of five other committees, viz. (1) the great men of the wards committee, (2) the great men of the fields committee, (3) the great men (numbering) two hundred, (4) the great men of the village committee, and (5) the great men of *udāsīna* committee [*Mad. Ep. Rep.*, 1904–5, part II, par. 7]. Again, no. 262 of 1913 in *Report* for 1913–14, p. 30, mentions another committee in each village, the land-survey committee, which had to classify lands according to their yielding capacity, and also to measure them. This committee was useful in connexion with the survey of land by government, as carried out, for instance, in the seventeenth year of Rājārāja I [*Mad. Ep. Rep.*, 1912–13, p. 96] and in the sixteenth of Kulottuṅga I (no. 317 of 1913 in *Report* for 1913–14, p. 37). The extent, ownership, assessment, classification of land (no. 262, ibid., stating eight classes of land), &c., were to be noted in the village and temple registers by specially appointed clerks, and both such registry and possession were deemed essential to establish ownership. No. 269 of 1912, in *Report* for 1912–13, p. 98, similarly mentions a committee to supervise cultivation and collect the produce called *ūrvāriyam*, while no. 257 of 1912 mentions *Amṛtagaṇattār* and *Gaṇapperumakkal*, as names of assemblies forming probably the executive committee of the village assembly [*Ep. Ind.*, vol. xi, p. 224], which is again referred to in nos. 302, 308, 312, and 315 of 1914.

A large number of Chola epigraphs reviewed in the *Madras Epigraphy Report* for 1915–16, p. 115, gives additional interesting details regarding the working of the village assemblies. The village of Brahmadeśam in a *taluk* of North Arcot district in which these epigraphs were found was an *agrahāra* with an organized village assembly, called *Gaṇapperumakkal Gaṇavāriyapperumakkal*, with many committees working under its control. One of them was a committee to manage the affairs of the village (*grāmakārya*), and another to manage those of the temple. The latter committee had an accountant entitled *Trairājyaghaṭikā-madhyasta*, 'the arbitrator of the college' (*ghaṭikā*) (named) *Trairājya* [see no. 194 of 1915 B, ibid., p. 18]. The grants recorded in nos. 192 and 194 are stated to have been entrusted by the *Mahā-Sabhā* to the great people of the *Gaṇavāriyam* doing duty in that year ('the members of the Samvatsara-vāriya who looked after the *Grāmakārya*') (according to no. 192), and if they failed in their duty it was stipulated that the *Śraddhāmantas* (i. e. those who interested themselves in the charity) should collect a fine from each member of that committee on behalf of the king. The assembly also evidently had under its control a body of *madhyastas* or arbitrators (no. 226 of 1915), who wrote the tank accounts and received for maintenance a fixed quantity of paddy, a pair of cloths, and some gold. 'In presenting accounts for audit by the assembly each of these was required to undergo the ordeal of holding the red-hot iron in his hand. If he came out safe and hence also pure, he would be presented with a bonus of one quarter of the surplus. If, on the other hand, he burnt his hand, and hence was in default, he would be fined 10 *kalañju*, without of course further bodily punishment inflicted upon him' [*Mad. Ep. Rep.*, 1915–16, p. 116]. No. 178 of 1915, ibid., p. 16, mentions the accountant of the *Samvatsara Vāriyam* committee, who was one of the signatories to an agreement into which the *mahāsabhā* entered.

It should be noted that committee members were expected to take an active part in the discussion of questions before the meetings. We have already seen how in an inscription from the Telugu country [see *ante*, p. 149] eloquence at committee assemblies is extolled as a special merit. The rules of debate are indicated in an inscription of the ninth century A. C., discovered in Tinnevelly, which forbids the persistent obstruction of the proceedings of the assembly by members saying 'nay, nay', to every proposal brought up before the assembly, and contains the further provision 'that those who do this, together with their supporters, will pay a fine of five *kāśu* on each item in which they have so behaved' [no. 423 of 1906, in *Report* for 1906–7]. We should note in this connexion the total number of members expected to form a meeting of the assembly. The number should be at least that of all the various sub-committees put together, which will thus come up to forty-two. I have found but one inscription [no. 466 of 1912, in *Report* for 1912–13] which incidentally indicates the number by mentioning a deed of gift signed by about fifty persons, evidently the members of the assembly.

It may be pertinent to refer in this connexion to other available evidence regarding the conduct of the meetings of assemblies. The most interesting and important evidence is set forth in some of the Pāli works regarding the proceedings of the meetings of the Buddhist religious assembly of the *saṅgha.*[1]

When Bhikkhus assembled in chapter became violent, quarrelsome, disputatious, and kept on wounding one another with sharp words, the dispute was to be settled by the vote of the majority.[2]

The votes were to be signified by tickets (as in the South Indian epigraphic evidence).

[1] A very good account of the evidence is given in the brilliant essay entitled 'An Introduction to Hindu Polity' contributed to the *Modern Review* (Calcutta), by Mr. K. P. Jayaswal, M.A. (Oxon.), Barrister-at-law, Tagore Professor of Law for 1917 in the Calcutta University.

[2] In the original we have '*yebhuyyasikāya*' = Sans. *yad-bhūyas-ikā*. 'It means putting to the vote and deciding by a majority; this is done by drawing tickets (*salākā*): a good orthodox priest must be selected as *salākāgāhāpaka*, or ticket-issuer, who should be careful to have the votes taken when there is a majority of the orthodox (*dhamma-vādī*).' [Vijesinha Mudliar, quoted by Childers.]

A 'taker of the voting tickets' was to be appointed. He should have the following five qualifications, viz. freedom from partiality, malice, folly, and fear, as well as knowledge of what votes have been taken and what have not been taken. 'Some able and discreet Bhikkhu' was to bring forward a motion (*ñatti*) that the Bhikkhu 'of such and such a name' should be appointed as taker of the voting tickets. The consent of the Bhikkhu proposed as the person to undertake the office was of course previously obtained. The motion was then placed before the house for its opinion. Those who approved of it were to keep silence. Those who were against it were to speak.

The 'taking of votes' (*salākagāhā*) was necessary in the case of a division. It was regarded as invalid in the following ten cases, viz.

(1) When the matter in dispute is trivial;

(2) When the case has not run its course (i.e. when the necessary preliminaries of submission to arbitration have not been carried out);

(3) When regarding the matter in dispute the Bhikkhus have not formally remembered or been formally called upon to remember, the offence;

(4) When the taker of votes knows that those whose opinions are not in accordance with the law will be in the majority, or

(5) Probably may be in the majority;

(6) When he knows that the voting will result in a schism in the *saṅgha*;

(7) When he is in doubt whether the voting will result in a schism in the *saṅgha*;

(8) When the votes are irregularly given;

(9) When all do not vote equally;

(10) When they do not vote in accordance with the view they really hold.

The above conditions, showing the solicitude felt for the purity, fairness, frankness, and freedom of the debate, are well worthy of observance at modern political and other meetings. The voting was not rushed, but a full opportunity was given to the house to understand the question at issue. Care was also taken that the voting represented the actual opinion of the voter, whose independence and conscientiousness were not allowed to be affected by any undue influence or considerations of partisanship. The only limitation upon the freedom of discussion and decision by the majority of votes was that imposed by certain fundamental religious considerations which formed the very basis of the brotherhood, and violations of which would imply the dissolution of the *saṅgha* or order itself. On such serious questions no voting was allowed, and the principle of the equality of votes of all members was not recognized simply because a difference of opinion on them would destroy that unity of the church which it was the aim by such free and frank discussions in meetings to strengthen and develop.

There was also the practice of appointing special committees to deal with difficult or intricate cases which were unfit to be dealt with by the general *saṅgha*. Such a committee or jury or commission was to consist of Bhikkhus 'possessed of ten qualities', mental and moral, including proficiency in the tradition and rules of the church as well as capacity to deal with legal questions. An instance of this proceeding is also recorded where 'the venerable Kevata laid a resolution before the *saṅgha* at Vesāli: "Let the venerable *saṅgha* hear me. Whilst we are discussing this legal question, there is both much pointless speaking, and no sense is clear in any single speech. If it seem meet to the *saṅgha*, let the *saṅgha* settle this legal question by referring it to a jury."[1] Again: "If it seem meet to the *saṅgha*, let the *saṅgha* delegate four Bhikkhus of the east and four Bhikkhus of the west (all named) to settle this question by reference. This is the resolution." Again: "Let the venerable *saṅgha* hear me. During the inquiry into this matter there has been much pointless talk among us, and the sense in any single

[1] *Tadi saṅghassa pattakallam* (i.e. is ready, *prāptakālam*), *saṅgho imam adhikaranam ubbāhikāya vupasameyya*. *Ubbāhikāya* is to be derived from *ud+vah*, meaning 'reference'. [*S. B. E.*, vol. XX, p. 50.]

utterance is not clear. The *saṅgha* delegates four Bhikkhus of the east and four Bhikkhus of the west to settle this question by reference. Whosoever of the venerable ones approves thereof, let him keep silence. The delegation is made accordingly. The *saṅgha* approves thereof. Therefore it is silent. Thus do I understand."' The *saṅgha* then appointed a Bhikkhu of ten years' standing as seat regulator to the Nera Bhikkhus (the eight referees) who were to take their seats in the order of their seniority. The duty of the seat-regulator (*āsana-praññāpaka*, आसनप्रज्ञापक) was to see that they were provided with the seats they required (usually mats or rugs) in the hall or grove where they met. In the present instance the sub-committee repaired to the Valīka Ārāma, 'a pleasant place, quiet and undisturbed', to 'settle the matter there'.

There also seem to have been some well-understood conditions required in order to make a meeting of the *saṅgha* itself valid. There must be present in the meeting 'as many Bhikkhus as are capable of taking part in the proceeding. The formal consent must be produced of those who are in a fit state to convey their consent. Those who are present must have lodged no objection (against any one of them taking part in the proceeding or perhaps against the proceedings which are being carried out.)' [1]

[1] See *Chullavagga*, IV. 9, 10, 14 on the whole subject.

Meetings of assemblies are referred to even in the Vedas. The *Ṛg-veda* [X. 71, 10] thus appreciates a successful speaker and debater: 'All friends are joyful in the friend who cometh in triumph, having conquered in the Assembly. He is their blame-averter, food provider, prepared is he and fit for deed of vigour.' The *Atharva-veda* [VII. 12. 4] thus refers to a piece of persuasive oratory arresting the attention of the audience: 'Whether your thoughts are turned away or bound and fastened here or there we draw them hitherward again: let your mind firmly rest on me.' In *Av.* II. 27, a speaker seeks the help of spells and magic herbs to stimulate his eloquence in debate (*prāś*) and overcome his rival debaters (*pratiprāśita*): 'May (my) foe by no means win (*ji*) the dispute; over-powering, overcoming art thou; smite the dispute of (my) counter-disputant; make them sapless, O herb' [अरसान् = नीरसान् शुष्ककण्ठान् वक्तुम् असमर्थान् or रसरहितवाक्यान, i. e. असंमतप्रलापिनः कुरु, i. e. make them dry-throated, incapable of speaking or devoid of sweetness of speech, hence make their speeches irrelevant, inconsistent, and incoherent (Sāyaṇa)]. In *Av.* VII. 12. 3 the debater prays to Indra for the palm and pre-eminence in the meeting of the assembly: 'I appropriate to myself all the power of knowledge and wisdom that belong to these members of the assembly: Indra, make me conspicuous in all this gathered assembly, so that I may monopolize its attention.'[1] The members were also anxious that their speeches should be free from impropriety and rudeness and always agreeable and fair and never foul [*Av.* VII. 12. 1]. They even prayed for forgiveness of any sins of omission or commission of which they might be guilty in their debates at meetings: 'Each fault in the assembly . . . that we have done . . . even of that sin, thou (*sūrya*) art the expiation' [the *White Yajur Veda*, XX. 17]. The respect for the meeting was also thus expressed: 'Homage to the assemblies and to you, Presidents of the assemblies' [ibid., XVI. 24.]

Like the Pāli evidence, the epigraphic evidence of South India is indicative of full attendance at meetings of the assemblies. In the *Mahā-parinibbānasutta* [I. 4] the Buddha tells Ānanda that 'so long as the Vajjians hold these *full* and *frequent* public assemblies, so long they may be expected not to decline but to prosper', so great was his appreciation of the efficacy of the national interest in such institutions. Similarly, an inscription of

[1] Sāyaṇa points out that Indra, being the Lord of speech, is prayed to for success in carrying the assembly [इन्द्रस्यैव वागनुशासनकर्तृत्वात् समाजयकर्म्मणि तस्यैव प्रार्थनम् ।]. The phrase मामिन्द्रं भगिनं कृणु is explained by him to mean भाग्ययुक्तम् or जययुक्तम् कुरु, i.e. सर्वामपि सभां मदेकवाक्यश्रवणपरा कुरु, i.e. make the whole assembly concentrate its attention upon my single speech.

Rājādhirāja of A. D. 1046 records a meeting of the assembly 'without a vacancy', a fact which is again repeated in an inscription dated in the fourth year of the reign of Rājendra Chola II [Hultzsch, *S. I. Ins.*, vol. III, pp. 57, 173].

Meetings of the assembly were of course held in the public hall of the village. In Vedic India the hall served as a meeting-place for social intercourse and general conversation, as also for debates and verbal contests [*Rv.* VI. 28, 6; VIII. 4, 9; *Av.* VII. 12, 2–3; also *Rv.* II. 24, 13 (*sabheya*)]. The hall was also used for dicing, presumably when the assembly was not transacting public business [*Rv.* X. 34, 6; *Av.* V. 31, 6; XII. 3, 46]; a dicer is called *sabhā-sthāṇu*, 'pillar of the assembly-hall', doubtless because of his constant presence there [*Vājasaneyi saṃhita*, XXX. 18; *Taittirīya Br.*, III. 4, 16, 1 with Sāyaṇa's note]. The administrative and judicial business of some of the autonomous clans of Buddhist India was carried out in public assembly, at which young and old were alike present in their common Mote-Hall (*santhāgāra*) at Kapilavastu. When King Pasenadi asked for one of the daughters of the Sākiya chiefs as his wife the Sākiyas discussed the proposition in their Mote-Hall. A new Mote-Hall was constructed at Kapilavastu whilst the Buddha was staying at the Nigrodhārāma in the Mahāvana near by. He was asked to inaugurate the building, and the opening ceremony was accompanied by a series of ethical discourses lasting through the night delivered by himself, Ānanda, and Moggallana [Rhys Davids, *Buddhist India*, 19, 20]. Similarly, the Licchavi assembly was composed of numerous members who are mentioned in the *Jātakas* as holding their meeting in a 'royal rest-house' [IV. 7–24], once to discuss a marriage proposal [IV. 145], and at another time to make arrangements for the reception of a prince of a neighbouring royal house [IV. 146]. In some of the *smṛtis* [e.g. *Bṛhaspati*] one of the duties of the village assemblies [called *samūha*] laid down is the maintenance of public halls, while in one of the Nāsik inscriptions cited above there occurs the expression *Nigama-sabhā*, or the town-hall where the charitable or religious endowments were publicly proclaimed, accepted by the guilds, and registered in their archives. Similar evidence is forthcoming in the South Indian inscriptions. One of the Ukkal inscriptions [no. 7 of *S. I. Ins.*, vol. III, p. 12] mentions the assembly meeting in the front hall of the Puvanimāṇikka-Viṣṇugṛiham in the village [Sans. *mukha-maṇḍapa*]. Three inscriptions copied at Nattam, a hamlet of Parameśvara-maṅgalam in the Chingleput district, refer to the hall [*Chatuśśālā*] known as Rājendraśolan in the village where the assembly used to meet [*Madras Epigraphy*

Report, 1912–13, p. 98]. In some other inscriptions is recorded a gift of a jewel-like hall (*Śālā*) at Kāndalūr by King Rājarāja Deva [*S. I. Ins.*, vol. I, nos. 40, 66, 146, and the *Koṅgu Chronicle*, p. 64]. In no. 653 of 1909 (*Report* for 1909–10) the assembly of a Brahmadīya village meet under a tamarind tree called *Rājendracholam*. In Tamil inscriptions we generally find village assemblies meeting either in a *maṇḍapa* built for the purpose or in a temple. 'The peculiar circumstances under which the Mahājanas of Pāvaikudi met under a tamarind tree reminds us of the village pīpal-tree with the big platform round it found in the centre of almost every hamlet in the Mysore country where questions concerning the village public are decided by the people gathered in the assembly' [*Madras Epigraphy Report*, 1909–10, p. 90]. No. 398 of 1913 [ibid., *Report* for 1913–14] mentions an assembly of a Brahmadeya village meeting in a hall called *Tiruvaraṅgadevan*. No. 178 of 1915 (*Report* for 1915–16) mentions the great assembly of Madhurāntaka-Chaturvedimaṅgalam including the young and the old meeting together in the big hall called *Śembiyanmahādevīpperumaṇḍapam*, built by Rājarāja I, evidently for the purpose of the meetings of the assembly.

We have now discussed the evidence of literature and inscriptions on the institutions through which the collective life and culture of the village were expressed, and on the way in which the village assemblies held their meetings and administered their affairs. We have also discussed the evidence of the Ukkal and Uttaramallūr inscriptions regarding the various committees instituted by the general assembly of the village to govern the manifold interests of communal life and the qualifications laid down for the membership of such committees. The evidence leads to the conclusion that these several committees were, legally speaking, sub-committees of the larger general assembly appointing them, rather than independent and unco-ordinated committees. Doubts on this point may be solved by a reference to the fact mentioned in the Uttaramallūr inscription that the casting of lots for election of committee members took place before 'a full meeting of the great assembly, including young and old', as well as all the priests to be found in the village on the day of the meeting. One of the Ukkal inscriptions again [no. 11] expressly refers to a meeting of 'the *great* assembly, including the great men elected for the year and the great men elected for the tank'. The superiority of the general assembly is further indicated by the fact that every member of the committees was bound to render 'an account of his stewardship' immediately before or after the expiry of his term of office.

The next question that suggests itself is, that if there was an independent and supreme assembly of the village, did it include all the residents as its members? We are indeed led to infer that it did from the passage quoted above about the *full* meeting of the assembly including the young and old members, and even the priestly outsiders who might happen to be present in the village on the occasion. Similarly, no. 178 of 1915, in *Report* for 1915–16, refers to a meeting of the great assembly, including the young and the old. But against this inference we have the positive testimony of an earlier inscription at Manūr in the Tinnevelly district [no. 423 of 1906, *Report* for 1906–7], dated in the thirty-fifth year of the reign of Mārañjadaiyan (i. e. about the ninth century A. C.), which lays down certain qualifications for membership of the *sabhā* or assembly, as the aforesaid inscriptions lay down those for membership of its committees. The very promulgation of such rules of membership implies that the assembly was not a universal body open to all the residents, but was a narrower, select, and restricted body open only to those who could qualify themselves for its membership according to the rules. Thus it is stated that

(1) Of the children of shareholders in the village, only one who is well-behaved and has studied the *Mantra-Brāhmaṇa* and one *Dharma* (i. e. code of

law) may be on the village assembly (*manru*) to represent the share held by him in the village, and only one person of similar qualifications may be on the assembly for a share purchased, received as present, or acquired by him as *strīdhana* (through his wife);

(2) Shares purchased, presented, or acquired as *strīdhana* could entitle one person, if at all, only to full membership in the assemblies; and in no case should quarter, half, or three-quarter membership be recognized;

(3) Those who purchase shares must elect only such men to represent their shares on the assembly as have critically studied a whole Veda with its *pariśiṣṭas*;

(4) Those who do not possess full membership as laid down by rule (2) cannot serve on any committee (*vāriyam*) (for the management of village affairs).

Thus the above conditions lay down a property qualification combined with a certain minimum of moral fitness and intellectual proficiency in legal and religious literature for every aspirant after a position in the general assembly of the village, while clause (4) insists on those qualifications (which are elaborated with the necessary fullness and additions only in the Uttaramallūr inscriptions) for candidates for membership of the assembly-committees.

It should further be noted that the rules laid down for assemblies in the aforesaid inscriptions refer only to those villages known as *Brahmadeya* (i. e. Brāhmaṇa), villages which were generally constituted by Brāhmaṇas, and designated *sabhās*. But besides such Brahmanical *sabhās* two other classes of assemblies are referred to in the South Indian inscriptions, viz. (1) the assemblies of all the residents of a village (*ūrom*) including cultivators and professionals, and (2) the assemblies or guilds of merchants (*nagarattom*).

A Brāhmaṇa village governed by its *sabhā* need not necessarily exclude other classes of inhabitants. No. 315 of 1909 (*Report* for 1909–10) refers to Brāhmaṇa villages (*agarabrahmadeśa*), agricultural villages and towns (*nagara*), as making a joint gift under compulsion. A typical Brāhmaṇa village is that recorded in no. 277 of 1913 (*Report* for 1913–14) in the thirteenth year of Jatāvarman Sundara-Pāṇḍya I, which is one of the few inscriptions mentioning the foundation of a new village, called in this case *Vikrama-Pāṇḍya-chaturvedi-maṅgalam*, where 108 Brahman families were settled on lands bought from the old title-holders and tenants, together with trees, wells, paths, channels, and embankments, showing the land-divisions. The central temple, the village library, the house-sites of the 108 Brāhmaṇas, of the librarians (*sarasvatī-bhaṇḍā-*

rattār), and of other village servants occupied 4 *veli* of land. The village servants were of various other castes, including drummer, potter, blacksmith, goldsmith, washerman, (each with a *vṛtti* of $\frac{1}{4}$), barber ($\frac{3}{8}$), watchman ($\frac{3}{4}$), servant ($\frac{1}{8}$), carpenter and accountant ($\frac{1}{2}$), and two doctors ($1\frac{3}{4}$). The Brāhmaṇas included teachers of Vedas (3) and of Sūtras (1), who were entitled each to a further grant of 1 *veli* of land for his maintenance. Land was also provided for grazing cattle, and a right of way was secured through other lands to a tank where the Brahmans could perform their daily prayers (*sandhyā vandana*). Thus even the typical Brāhmaṇa village with its public temple, library, grazing grounds, &c., accommodated artisans and men of other classes and castes as well. No. 278 of 1913 (*Report* for 1913–14) refers to a similar grant of 116 *velis* of land to the typical number of 108 Brāhmaṇas, who were bound to bless the king on *Śrībali* days.

CHAPTER VIII

SOME IMPORTANT CORPORATIONS

As has been already stated, villages and assemblies other than those constituted by the Brāhmaṇas alone also existed. We shall deal with those of merchants first. No. 349 of 1912 (*Report* for 1912–13, p. 99) from Vīralūr in the North Arcot district, assigned to the time of Rājarāja I, refers to a gift by a guild of *nānādeśī* (merchants), literally, those who come from or have dealings with various countries. But an inscription from Basinikoṇḍa in the Chittoor district refers to certain merchant-guilds, which apparently had been flourishing from very early times with an organization that established their influence over allied communities in distant parts of India [no. 342 of 1912, *Report* for 1912–13]. The record relates that the community, consisting of *nāḍu*, *nagara*, and *nānādeśī*, met in a special congregation at Śirāvalli, comprising 1,500 representatives of all *samayas* (religious denominations) coming from the four and eight quarters as well as of their followers of various sects and tenets. The object of the conference was to declare

Śirāvalli a Nānādeśīya-Daśamaḍi-Erivīrapattana, and to confer certain privileges on the town. Such privileges were perhaps similar to those mentioned in another inscription assigned to the time of Rājendra-Chola I [no. 256 of 1912, *Report* for 1912–13)], which gives some interesting details regarding the same merchant guild. It states that the guild were praised by 500 *vīra-śāsanas* (i.e. edicts ?) for their deeds, were protectors of the Valañjiya religion and devotees of Bhaṭṭārikā (i. e. Durgā ?), and comprised various sub-divisions coming from the 1,000 districts of the four quarters, the 18 towns, the 32 *velarpuram*, and the 64 *ghātikā-sthāna.* These *Nānādeśīs* met together at Mayilārpura (i. e. Mylapore) and decided to convert Kāttur, which was originally *Ayyapulal* into a *Vīrapaṭṭiṇa*, and thus to exempt its inhabitants from all communal contributions, entitling them to receive twice what they used to get previously (in the matter of honorary privileges perhaps). They resolved also that henceforward the town was not to be inhabited by such members of the mercantile classes as (1) demanded taxes or tolls by threatening people with drawn swords or by capturing them, and (2) wantonly deprived people of their food or otherwise afflicted them. They also declared that those who offended against this decision were placed outside the Valañjiya community (i. e. were excommunicated).

A record from Baligāmi in the Mysore state supplies also a very long eulogy of these merchants and states, in addition to what has been stated in the Kāṭṭūr epigraph, that they were heroes (*vīras*), born to wander over many countries ever since the beginning of the Kṛta age, penetrating regions of the six continents by land and water routes and dealing in various articles such as horses, elephants, precious stones, perfumes, and drugs either wholesale or retail [*Ep. Carn.*, vol. VII, Sk. 118; and *Madras Epigraphy*, 1912–13, p. 100]. This boast of the mercantile community is justified by the existence of stone records even in Ceylon and Burma which refer to their communal gifts in those countries. The Vaiṣṇava temple at Pagan in Upper Burma was built by the merchants (*nānādeśī*) of that town [*Ep. Ind.*, vol. VII, p. 197].

Similarly, no. 88 of 1914 (*Report* for 1914–15, p. 104) in the tenth year of Jaṭāvarman Vīra Pāṇḍya refers to an assembly of merchants, important like the Hansa League, from 18 sub-divisions of 79 districts meeting together in a conference in which they decide to set apart the income derived from merchandise for repairs to a temple, e. g. $\frac{1}{4}$ *paṇam* on each bundle of female cloths, each *podi* of pepper, areca-nuts, and on each gold piece, and the like.

But besides these Hansa Leagues of merchants, there were also other assemblies of certain special communities which from their numerical strength attained to a great measure of political importance. These were the assemblies of:

(1) The *Velaikkāras* consisting of working classes No. 600 of 1912 (*Report* for 1912–13) records a shrine being placed under them, and they agreed to 'protect the villages belonging to the temple, its servants, property, and devotees, even though, in doing this, we lose ourselves or otherwise suffer. We provide for all the requirements of the temple so long as our community continues to exist, repairing such parts of the temple as get dilapidated in the course of time, and we get this our contract which is attested by us engraved on stone and copper so that it may last as long as the moon and sun endure.' The community was led by the Valañjiyar and Nagarattār sub-sects of merchants who extended their trade all over the country, and are represented by the present Baṇajiga and Nagartta communities of the Kanarese country who are mostly Liṅgāyat Śaivas and Vaiṣṇavas respectively. The Velaikkāras emigrated into Ceylon and formed a body of mercenaries employed by the Sinhalese kings. They are also mentioned in the Tanjore inscriptions of the Chola kings, of whose army they formed a part [*Mad. Ep. Report*, 1912–13, p. 102].

(2) The *Iḍaṅgai* community of 98 sub-sects. No. 489 of 1912 (*Madras Epigraphy*, 1912–13,

p. 109) registers a compact drawn up on their behalf by the Śrutimans. of Uṭṭattūr (who were probably a sect of cultivators of the Iḍaṅgai community) assembled in the *maṇḍapa* of the temple, called Uttamasolan. The compact was to the following effect: 'We, the members of the 98 subsects, enter into a compact in the fortieth year of King Kulottuṅga Chola III, that we shall hereafter behave like the sons of the same parents, and what good or evil may befall any one of us will be shared by all. If anything derogatory happens to the Iḍaṅgai class we will jointly assert our rights till we establish them. Those who behave differently from the rules shall not be recognized as Srutimans' [*Mad. Ep. Report*, 1912–13, p. 109]. As regards their distinguishing symbols it is stated: 'It is also understood that only those who during their congregational meetings to settle communal disputes display the *birudas* of horn, bugle, and parasol shall belong to our class. Those who have to recognize us now and hereafter in public must do so from our distinguishing symbols—the feather of the crane and the loose-hanging hair. The horn and the conch-shell shall also be sounded in front of us and the bugle blown according to the fashion obtaining among the Iḍaṅgai people' [ibid.]. A later record from Āḍutarai in the Trichinopoly district [no. 34 of 1913, App. C, in *Madras Epigraphy*, 1912–13] refers again to the Valaṅgai 98 classes and the Iḍaṅgai 98 classes who enter into an agreement among themselves against the Brāhmaṇas and other landlords who oppressed them. Similarly, nos. 59, 361, and 362 of 1914 (in *Madras Epigraphy*, 1914–15, p. 106) register an agreement entered into by the assembly of Parāntakanāḍu and the Valaṅgai 98 and Iḍaṅgai 98 sub-sects regarding payment of certain dues to the king or temple [A. D. 1429–30].

(3) The *Valaṅgai* community of 98 sub-sects as referred to in the inscriptions nos. 34 of 1913, App. C, and 59, 361, 362 of 1914 noticed above.

(4) The *Pallis* referred to in no. 35 of 1913 (in *Madras Epigraphy*, 1912–13). They rescued the images of gods and 63 devotees (*nāyanmārs*) which were being carried away to Dvārasamudra (Halebīd), and agreed to provide for the necessary upkeep for their worship, viz. 100 *kalam* of rice and 5,000 *kāśu*. They collected this amount by levying on each family a tax of 1 *kuruni* of rice and 50 *kāśu*, which they realized, if necessary, by 'taking away vessels, breaking pots and beating them'. For this voluntary act of self-sacrifice for and service to the temple the Pallis were honoured in the temple by special privileges and presentation of silk cloths. These coercive measures were of course permitted by the king. No. 368 of 1914 (*Madras Epigraphy*, 1914–15) also refers to three classes of Pallis included

in an assembly representing various groups of people.

(5) The *Ayyapolil* guild of merchants, consisting of 500 members with their organization extending almost throughout Southern India, as indicated in a record in the reign of Vikramachola [no. 97 of 1915 and *Mad. Ep. Rep.*, 1916, p. 121].

(6) The Vaiśyas of the *Kuveravaṁśa,* devotees of Śiva and Viṣṇu, with many branches, whose chief object in life was the maintenance of *dharma*, and whose members were noted for their charities, such as construction of temples, tanks, wells, and water-sheds, planting of groves, patronage of poets, &c. [*Mad. Ep. Rep.*, 1916, p, 151].

(7) The Deśi-merchants of the Kubera lineage referred to in nos. 15, 16 of 1916, App. C, 'whose sole delight was distribution of food to the needy, the orphans, and the suppliant beggars'. To the temple of Deśīśvara they made a communal gift of a fixed fee on all the articles in which they traded, such as musk, saffron, yak-tail, cus-cus, cotton, cotton-thread, beads, sealing-wax, areca, rock-salt, wax, resin, hemp, wool, camphor, sandal, silk-thread, tiger-skin, women's cloths, lead, and tin. The form of this remarkable gift points not only to the efficiency of the machinery for the collection of these taxes on the profits of trade in a variety of articles, but also to commercial progress and

economic prosperity, as implied in the very volume of that trade supporting taxation on its profits.

Like the merchant-guilds noticed above, there were also some important organizations of craft-guilds. No. 261 of 1909 refers to the guild of oil-mongers of Kāñchi and its suburbs, and also those of twenty-four *nagaras*, who met in a temple of Kāñchimānagar, and decided that the usual tax on oil-mills in the temple premises at Tirukkacchūr should be paid to the temple together with a specified quantity of oil and a voluntary fee of one *kāśu* per oil-mill. This decision they agreed to observe as *jātidharma*, i. e. duty which every member owed to his caste. The taxes which were thus assigned by the assembly of oil-mongers in favour of the Tirukkacchūr temple were not what they had ordinarily to pay to government, but what their spontaneous offerings diverted from application to communal purposes.

There were again some remarkable examples of seamen's guilds. One of these is referred to in the Moṭṭupalli record of the Kākatīya sovereign Gaṇapatideva-Mahārāja [no. 600 of 1909, *Madras Epigraphy*, 1909–10] who grants a charter (*abhaya-śāsana*) to merchants trading in their vessels from the seaport of Moṭṭupalli with islands and coast towns in distant countries. The necessity for the charter was that kings of old used to confiscate by force all the cargo, gold, elephants, horses, precious stones, &c., of vessels *en route* from one country to another, which, driven by contrary winds, happened to be stranded and wrecked in the sands near Moṭṭupalli. 'Seeing that protection (of my subjects) is far more important (to me) than my life', says Gaṇapati, 'we have remitted out of compassion all (taxes) except *kūpaśulka* on these enterprising (merchants) trading on sea in order to secure fame and to maintain the principles of a righteous government.' The inscription gives the details of the *kūpaśulka* akin to the modern custom-house duties. They comprised fees on sandal-wood, country (?)-camphor, China-camphor, pearls, rose-water, ivory, civet (*javādu*), camphor-oil (*karpūra-taila*), copper, zinc, *riseya* (resin ?), lead, silk-thread, corals, perfumes, pepper, and areca-nuts. This long list of cargo shipped by the merchant-men of the Moṭṭupalli seamen supports the glowing appreciation and description of Marco Polo of the trade at the port of Mutfili (identified with Moṭṭupalli), which he visited during the reign of the Kākatīya queen Rudramadevī, about the end of the thirteenth century A. C.

There seems to have been a renewal and amendment of this charter a century later in the reign of Annapota-Reḍḍi [mentioned in no. 601 of 1909] who permitted 'the merchants of Moṭṭupalli who traded with distant islands and coast-towns to stop at their will in their homes at Moṭṭupalli and to leave them for other places (without any official pressure). He also remitted the tax called *aputtirika-daṇḍam* on foreign merchants (who traded in his dominions). Further, the duties on gold and silver were abolished; a third of the export duty on sandal was remitted, and merchants were allowed the liberty to sell their goods brought from other shores to anybody under any conditions, and to carry in exchange likewise to other countries any goods they chose. It was proclaimed that henceforward no cloths would be detained in the warehouse (?), and tolls on other articles would under no circumstances be different from what they were before.' The following rates of duty were fixed:

(A) Goods coming from the southern side—on 100 (packages) of import 3 (packages), and on 100 cloths of export 2 coins (?).

(B) Goods coming from the north—on 100 packages of import 5, and on 100 cloths of export 3 coins (?).

(C) Goods exported to foreign islands—3 coins (?) on 100 cloths;

(D) $7\frac{1}{2}$ (?) on 100 pearls.[1]

[1] 'It is curious to note that this interesting record is written in both the Tamil and Telugu languages. It is not unlikely that the reason is to be sought for in the fact that the majority of the

Among other minor and sundry kinds of assemblies we may notice that of the Bhattas of Rājāśraya-chaturvedi-maṅgalam referred to in no. 479 of 1908 (*Madras Epigraphy*, 1908–9) which records that this learned assembly laid down on the authority of Gautama, Bodhāyana, Kauṭilya, and Yājñavalkya the profession to be followed by the *anuloma* sect called the Rathakāras. This epigraph thus shows that questions of castes and professions were settled at the beginning of the thirteenth century A. C. by learned assemblies on the authority of past teachers. Secondly, we may instance the composite assembly of various groups of people, including three classes of Pallis, four or six sub-divisions of professionals, artisans, and other castes as referred to in no. 368 of 1914 (*Madras Epigraphy*, 1914–15).

merchants whom this charter concerned were, perhaps, Tamils, whose capabilities as sailors from very early times have been proved beyond doubt by the series of conquests on sea registered in the eulogistic introductions to the records of the great Chola kings, Rājarāja I and Rājendra-Chola I. The Telugu version of the epigraph [No. 602 of 1909] supplies the additional information that the pillar on which this charter to the sea-merchants is engraved was set up under orders of the minister Somayāmātya in the town of Mukulā, which was probably a surname either of Moṭṭupalli itself or of one of its suburbs.' [*Mad. Ep. Report*, 1909–10, pp. 107, 118.]

CHAPTER IX

§ I

PUBLIC INSTITUTIONS

We have now considered the subject of local government in ancient India in all its aspects on the basis of our available evidence, but our study will be incomplete without a reference to the growth of the various kinds of public institutions, which was one of the most remarkable characteristics of communal life proving the success, to some extent, of the indigenous administration. We have already referred to the existence of public halls in the villages and towns of ancient India, where meetings of the assembly and other public functions were held. But besides these halls there were also other kinds of public buildings and institutions which may be noted in this connexion. One inscription registers the gift to a temple of a *maṭha* (= a college) in the western street for reciting the Veda [ibid., p. 125]. Another refers to the *maṭha* of Āṇḍār Sundara-Perumāl at Kāñchipuram [ibid., p. 123]. A third inscription [ibid., p. 86] registers the gift of one house and a house-garden of 41 feet for purposes of a *maṭha*, together with some land mortgaged to it as a guarantee for regular supply of rice. 'The succession of pupils (of the donee) shall enjoy this *maṭha* as long as the moon and the sun endure.' An inscription attributed to Kṛṣṇa III of the Rāṣṭrakūṭa dynasty [A. D. 940–56] mentions fines payable into court called *dharmāsana* [ibid., vol. III, p. 12]. An inscription of the eastern Chalukya dynasty mentions two *sattras* (i. e. almshouses for Brāhmaṇas [*S. I. Ins.*, vol. I, p. 61], and another speaks of a *maṇḍapa* 'which was to be used as a water-shed and *sattram*' [ibid., p. 136]. No. 465 of 1909 (*Mad. Ep. Rep.*, 1910, p. 41), assigned to Kulasekhara I, records a gift of two villages for a Vaiṣṇava *Maṭha*, where learned Brāhmaṇas from eighteen Vaiṣṇava countries were to be fed. No. 181 of 1912 refers to a *maṭha-pati*, who is an important functionary frequently appearing on temple councils in later records. No. 509 of 1912 (*Mad. Ep. Rep.*, 1913, p. 57) records a sale of land belonging to a temple for a *maṭha*. An interesting series of inscriptions from the Kurnool district, assigned to the middle of the thirteenth century A.C., refers to a famous *maṭha* named Golaki maṭha, which is stated to have wielded its spiritual influence over three lacs of villages under a succession of famous teachers. Another important *maṭha* was that of the *Mahāvratins* mentioned in no. 423 of 1914 (*Mad. Ep. Rep.*, 1915, p. 42). A series of epigraphic records in South India relates to *maṭhas* connected with Śaivism, which grew in power and popularity under the Chola kings, so that by the thirteenth century we notice a number of them under Śaiva Sannyāsins influencing the greater part of the Tamil country. No. 467 of 1908 refers to a *maṭha* called Tiruvāgīśam-Rajendraśolan at Tirucchattimuram, and another *maṭha* at Śembaikkuḍi [*Mad. Ep. Report*, 1908–9, p. 103]. Other *maṭhas* connected with the *Śivayogins* or *Māhesvaras* are mentioned in nos. 164, 177, 402, 583 of 1908. Besides the *maṭha* there was also another institution called *guhai*, or a monastery. No. 471 of 1912 records the gift of such a monastery for a Śaiva saint by a village which also provided for the feeding of all strangers who might visit it. The property of this monastery was confiscated in the twenty-second year of Kulottuṅga Chola III, when there was a general crusade against these non-Brahmanical Śaiva *maṭhs* instigated by the Brāhmaṇas. The *maṭhs* were not, however, altogether suppressed, since we find them flourishing in the time of Rājarāja III.

Villages had not only their public halls and temples, *maṭhas*, and monasteries, but also schools of learning. One of the most interesting of such schools is mentioned in no. 202 of 1912 (*Mad. Ep. Rep.*, 1912–13, p. 110), which registers the generous gift of a donor who assigned some land for the maintenance of a grammar-hall in the temple at Tiruvorraiyūr called '*Vyākaraṇa-dāna-Vyākhyāna maṇḍapa*, for the upkeep of the teachers and pupils who should study grammar there, and for the worship of the god *Vyākaraṇa-dāna-Perumal* (i. e. Śiva), who in that very *maṇḍapa* was pleased to appear before Pāṇini-Bhagavān for fourteen continuous days and to teach him the first fourteen aphorisms (with which Pāṇini's grammar begins) known as Māheśwar Sūtras'. This famous school of grammar is referred to in other later records. No. 110 of 1912, assigned to the thirteenth year of Sundara Pāṇḍya-Deva III, registers an agreement by which the residents of Pular-Kottan submit to a special tax levied in the northern and southern divisions of Tiruvorraiyūr for maintaining the same historic *maṇḍapam* and other similar buildings of the temple. No. 201 of 1912 in the thirty-eighth year of Kulottuṅga Chola III, registers the gift by a private person of a village for the upkeep of the same grammar-hall, and refers to the king's declaration making the village rent-free. No. 120 of 1912 again registers the king's gift of a village and some gold ornaments to the god Vyākaraṇa-dāna Perumal at the instance of a female devotee, the king being

Kulottuṅga Chola III. One of the temple priests was also called Vyākaraṇa-dāna-bhaṭṭa after the god Śiva, who 'gave' grammar to Pāṇini.

Similarly, no. 182 of 1915 refers to the benefactions of a Vaiśya named Mādhava, who constructed the surrounding halls of a temple, and also a *maṇḍapa* called Jananātha-maṇḍapa where, by the royal grant of Vīrarājendra-deva (A. D. 1062), were established (1) a school for the study of the Vedas, Śāstras, Grammar, *Rūpāvatāra* (probably name of a grammatical work recently discovered), &c., (2) a hostel for students, and (3) a hospital. The students were provided with food, bathing-oil on Saturdays, and with oil for lamps. The hospital was named Vīra-śolan (*scil.* Vīra Chola), and provided with fifteen beds for sick people. The staff and establishment for the school-hostel and hospital comprised one physician in whose family the privilege of administering medicines was hereditary, one surgeon, two servants who fetched drugs, supplied fuel, and did other services for the hospital, two maidservants for nursing the patients, and one general servant for the hostel and hospital. Among the medicines stored in the hospital are mentioned *āśā-harītaki*, *gomūtra-harītaki*, *bhallātaka-harītaki*, *bilvādi-ghṛtam*, *vajra-kalpam*, *kalyāṇa-lavaṇam*, and some varieties of *tailam* or oils—medicines which are still in use under the indigenous medical systems of the land.

This is probably one of the best pieces of available evidence on the schools, hostels, and hospitals of ancient India [see *Mad. Ep. Rep.* for 1916, p. 119].

No. 518 of 1915 similarly registers the gift of a Chālukyan queen to the 140 *mahājanas* of a village belonging to her for 'the maintenance of a feeding-house (*sattra*), the commentator (on *śāstras*), the reader of the *Purāṇas*, and the teacher of the *Ṛg-Veda* and *Yajur-Veda* to students.

Another most remarkable example of secular charities, of the establishment of a school, a hospital, and a feeding-house, is recorded in a huge pillar inscription at Malkāpuram in the Guntūr taluk of the Guntūr district, which 'is of very great interest both for the historical information it supplies regarding the Kākatīya kings and for the detailed account which it gives of the famous Pāśupata teachers who preceded Viśveśvara-Śivāchārya of the Gauḍa country, who was himself the royal preceptor and a highly learned scholar' [*Mad. Ep. Rep.*, 1917, p. 122]. This celebrated religious leader used one of the many royal gifts bestowed upon him to found at Mandaram (the present Mandadam) all the institutions necessary for the commonweal, viz. temple, monastery, feeding-house, settlement of families of (Drāviḍa) Brāhmaṇas, schools of students of Śaiva Puritans, together with a maternity and a hospital. Three teachers were appointed for teaching the three Vedas, and five for logic, literature, and the *āgamas*. There were also appointed one doctor and one accountant (Kāyastha). For the *maṭha* and feeding-house were provided six Brāhmaṇa servants. Village-guards called *Vīrabhadras* were also appointed, together with village craftsmen called *Vīramuṣṭis*, who had to perform the duties of goldsmith, coppersmith, mason, bamboo-worker, blacksmith, potter, architect, carpenter, barber, and artisan. In the feeding-house arrangements were made for the feeding at all times of men of *all* castes from the Brāhmaṇa down to the Chaṇḍāla—a remarkable instance of toleration and catholicity worthy of the creed followed by the donor. It was also directed that the presiding teacher appointed to supervise these charities should be liable to removal for neglect of duty or misconduct by the entire Śaiva community (*sāntānikā*). There are other inscriptions to show that the same strict regulations applied to Śaiva teachers appointed as heads of *maṭhas* [ibid., and *Ep. Ind.*, vol. XII, p. 290 f.].

§ 2

EFFICIENCY OF ORGANIZATION

We have now considered the growth of local administration in ancient India in its various aspects and spheres of activity, together with the machinery of government evolved to cope with the manifold interests of communal life in ordinary and normal times and situations. But the test of the efficiency of a government lies in its capacity to deal with extraordinary circumstances and abnormal situations and to develop a proper degree of public spirit in the governed. There are numerous proofs and instances on record which will enable us to conclude that, judged by those two tests of government and the criteria of its efficiency, our ancient system of local administration will not be found to be wanting or to break down. In trying times and exceptional situations, such as those of a famine for example, we find that the assemblies rise to the occasion and to a full sense of their responsibilities in that regard. A South Indian inscription of about A. D. 1054, for instance, records how a village, being visited by a famine, the assembly of the village, expecting no succour from the king, themselves moved in the matter of securing relief for the people. They secured a loan of 1011 *kalañju* of gold and 464 *palam* of silver in jewellery and vessels from the local temple to which they mortgaged 8¾ *veli* of the common lands of the village, from the produce of which the interest on the loan was to be paid [*Mad. Ep. Rep.*, 1899–1900, p. 20]. Another case of famine is reported in the reign of Kulottuṅga Chola III in inscriptions nos. 274 and 279 of 1909

(*Mad. Ep. Rep.*, 1909–10, p. 95) when the assembly of Tirukkacchūr borrowed 15 *kāśu* of a generous individual, and for interest gave him a piece of land belonging to the whole village, the government dues on which they themselves paid. Thus where there was even no remission of taxes by government the assembly were more mindful of their duties. The private person was a generous donor who provided for temple worship, seeing it was neglected during the time of the famine. No. 397 of 1913 also records a similar case of famine, or 'bad time and scarcity of grain', and loan arranged by the assembly to tide over the difficulty, borrowed from the temple treasury amounting to 60 *kāśu* with interest at 2 *tūṇi* and 3 *kuruni* of paddy on 1 *kāśu*. No. 353 of 1909 records another interesting case. Rājendra Deva (A.D. 1052) paid some gold to an assembly for building a stone temple. They had built five *aṅgas* of the temple for half the money when famine occurred and the assembly could neither complete it nor return the money. The temple authorities complained against them, and the assembly was eventually let off on supplying an image of God found wanting in the temple. This is another case of royal indifference, contrasted with the assembly's concern in the matter of the popular weal.

Most of the famines mentioned relate to the time

of the decline of Chola power towards the latter part of the reign of Kulottuṅga III, who reigned from about A.D. 1287 to 1327, when there was considerable unrest in the country. One of the signs of that unrest or unsettlement is indicated in no. 264 of 1913 (*Mad. Ep. Rep.*, 1913–14, p. 30), which registers the gift of a lamp, oil, and wick to be provided out of the interest on 1,100 *kāśu* deposited only for a fixed period of five years and not permanently, so that the assembly had to produce the amount of the deposit every five years before it was renewed. This condition betrays a want of confidence and a sense of insecurity due to the weakening of the central authority in the country. Even temples had to part with their jewellery to pay for the cost of erecting certain necessary structures during those days of famine in the reign of Kulottuṅga III [see no. 458 of 1913]. In such hard times it is refreshing to observe proofs that the local administration did not break down. When the strong arm of a vigorous central government was withdrawn, we find a local administrative body stepping forward to afford full protection to the people under its charge in the disturbed state of the country. No. 273 of 1914 states that 'the assembled people (*nāḍu*) of *Valla-nāḍu* declared that thenceforward they will afford protection to the cultivators residing within the four boundaries of the sacred village of Tiruvaraṅgulam and its *devadāna* villages. If in the course of this protection any one of the assembly was found to rob, capture the cows of the cultivators, or do other mischief to them, the assembly agreed to assign two *mā* of wet land to the temple by way of fine for the offence committed' [*Mad. Ep. Rep.*, 1914–15, p. 99].

Besides their capacity to cope with difficult situations, the indigenous local administrations must also be credited with producing a high level of public spirit in the citizens. We have even some instances in which the public spirit or patriotism becomes a passion leading to extremes. No. 411 of 1912, assigned to the eighth year of Rājarāja (about A.D. 992) I, records that 'a certain Kalipperumān lost his life in the act of affording protection against ruin to his native village. Perhaps he sacrificed his life voluntarily, or in defending the village against an invading enemy. The good residents of the district in which Marudāḍu was situated provided for a permanent lamp to burn in the temple of Perundirukkoyil-Ālvār at that village in order to secure merit for the martyr' [*Mad. Ep. Rep.*, 1912–13, p. 96]. Here the patriotism of the individual has been rewarded by the gratitude and abiding recognition of his community which immortalized, by a monument more enduring than brass, the memory of a man who gave up his life for them. Another notable instance of individual service and communal appreciation is recorded in nos. 119 and 120 of 1908. The temple of Tiruttaliyāṇḍa-Nāyanār at Tirupputūr is stated in those records to have been occupied by the encamped Muhammadans (probably under Malik Kāfūr in A.D. 1310), and to have been consequently ruined and desecrated. The inhabitants of Tirupputūr were therefore very much unsettled. At this juncture a certain Viśālayadevar of Kuraikkuḍi, surnamed Avaiyan Periyanāyanār, reconsecrated the temple and saved the people apparently from imminent moral and religious degradation. 'The villagers of Tirupputūr, of their free will, agreed among themselves to show their gratitude to Viśālayadeva by assigning to him a specified quantity of corn from the harvest reaped by each individual and to confer on him certain privileges in the temple of Tiruttaliyāṇḍa-Nāyanār [ibid., 1908–9, pp. 82, 83]. Some inscriptions from the Madakasira taluk of the Anantapur district, ranging over a long period from the early ninth century, illustrate the heroic sacrifices of certain 'village Hampdens' and the grateful appreciation of the villagers concerned. No. 479 of App. B of 1916 mentions the case of a villager successfully repelling two or three destructive raids for which he was rewarded by a grant of land. No. 753, ibid., mentions the death of both son and father in a battle for their village. No. 17 of App. C of 1916 records the fame of a village warrior who defended his village against attacks. A heroic fight is described in no. 33 of App. C, in which the hero is said to have dispersed the attacking army of 1 lac (?) infantry and 1,000 horse, and killed 500 men and 100 horse. Nos. 19 and 58 of App. C mention a rent-free grant of land as the reward of blood spilt in the cause of protecting the community or village (all the above inscriptions are in *Mad. Ep. Rep.*, 1916–17). In this connexion we may refer to the *vīrgals* or hero-stones of Mysore, which mostly record grants of land in addition to commemorating the deaths of heroes. An inscription on the Begūr stone and also a sculpture found in the Bangalore taluk record the death of the commander of the Nāgattara troops in a battle that was fought between the forces of Ayyapadeva and those of Vīramahendra, and also the appointment of his successor and grant of villages to him [A. D. 908–38; see *Ep. Ind.*, vol. VI, p. 45]. A second clause in the supplementary inscription on the Ātakūr stone of A. D. 949–50 [see ibid., p. 57] gives another instance of a grant of villages in recognition of bravery in the battle-field to a hero who fought and survived, and we further learn from this record that grants of this kind were sometimes accompanied by the ceremony of washing the warrior's sword, just as religious grants were usually accompanied by the ceremony of laving the feet of the priest into whose hands the donation was actually given [Fleet, in *Imp. Gaz.*, 1908, vol. II, p. 60]. The Ablūr stone of about A. D. 1219 in the Dharwār district commemorates the death of the brothers Mācha and Goma fighting valiantly to repel a cattle-raid against their village led by Īśvaradeva of Belagavatti, modern Belagutti, in the Honnāli taluk of the Shimoga district [*Ep. Ind.*, V, 262]. The tablets of Kil-Muttugūr, Ambūr (villages in N. Arcot district), Naregal (Dharwār district), and Baṅgavādi (Kolar district) similarly preserve the memory of other village heroes who sacrificed themselves in repelling cattle-raids [*Ep. Ind.*, vol. IV, 178, 182, 183; vol. VI, 162; VII. 22]. Many other cases might be cited.

But the public spirit of the people generally flowed along other and diverse channels. It determined the character of the communal assembly also. Both the assembly as a collective body and the individual members often vied with one another for the promotion of the public good. To the public spirit, patriotism, and religious sense of both parties the villages owed all their public institutions in which were centred the intellectual and spiritual life of the community. The religious spirit decorated the villages with new temples and shrines; created liberal endowments for their repairs, maintenance, and development; and made provision for the multifarious necessaries and accessories of worship elaborated or sometimes invented by a pious imagination. It is difficult indeed to enumerate the manifold forms assumed by the popular religious offering. The commonest form repeatedly evidenced in numerous epigraphic records was the provision of the sacred lamp eternally burning before the gods of the temples, implying the provision of a perennial supply of the necessary oil and wick. Sometimes improvement was made upon that by the provision of camphor lamps. In other cases the piety of the people loved to associate itself with a more direct service to the gods: some took charge of their food, creating the necessary endowments for its eternal provision; others concerned themselves with the supply of the proper bathing-water, worthy of the deity, for which the necessary scents were permanently assured; others interested themselves in the gods' anointing; others were more anxious to assure that the processions of gods on festival days should always be carried out with due dignity and pomp, and must be under no risk of discontinuance due to want of funds; in others, again, the pious imagination seized upon the beat of drums at festivals as the fittest form of worship that could be offered. We have already cited the inscriptions recording these various forms of devout offering. There are again cases in which the gift of provision for processions is followed up by that for procession paths. No. 45 of 1914 (*Mad. Ep. Rep.*, 1914–15, p. 13), of Rājarāja II, found at Tiruppanandāl, records a grant of land for laying out a road called *Rājagambhīran-tiruvidi* for the god to pass through to the river Kollidam for the sacred bath festival. The inscription adds that 750 coco-nut trees were to be planted and cherished on both sides of the new road, and the income derived from them to be spent on providing lights and sundry other expenses in the temple. Similarly, no. 66 of 1913, App. C (*Mad. Ep. Rep.*, 1912–13, p. 77), of Kulottuṅga Chola III refers to lands purchased by a private individual for the purpose of laying out a road through which was to be carried in procession the image of Śirāla-Pillayār from the shrine of Śiruttoṇḍadeva at Tirucchen-gāttāṅgudi to the village Marugal. These lands were removed from the list of taxable lands under orders of the king. No. 397 of 1914 (*Mad. Ep. Rep.*, 1914–15, p. 40), again, records the collective gift by about twenty-five individuals of a temple, a golden shrine, stone and metallic images of gods, together with provision for processions, and the construction of a water-shed and well for the use of devotees, with the assignment of sufficient lands for the upkeep of the aforesaid charities. Sometimes, again, the offering took the more useful form of providing for the recital of the *Mahābhārata* for the edification of a village [no. 163 of 1909 (*Mad. Ep. Rep.*, 1909–10, p. 19)]. There are again instances of public amusements being provided for in connexion with the temples. No. 65 of 1914 (*Mad. Ep. Rep.*, 1914–15, p. 16) records a gift of land by the great assembly of Kāmaravalli-chaturvedi-maṅgalam to Śākkai Mārāyan Vikramaśolan for performing the dance (*Sākkaikūttu*) thrice on each of the festivals *Mārgalitiruvādirai* and *Vaigāsitiruvādirai*. No. 253 of 1914 again records a similar gift of land to a lady for giving nine performances of dancing before the god at Tiruveṅgavāśal in the fourteenth year of Vikrama-Chola. It may be noted that such public amusements were also encouraged by the kings. Rājarāja I instituted the representation on the stage of a drama entitled *Rājarājesvarī nāṭaka* [*South Ind. Ins.*, vol. II, p. 306]. No. 211 of 1912 (*Mad. Ep. Rep.*, 1912–13, p. 29) records the personal attendance of Rājarāja III at a singing party in the *Rājarājan maṇḍapa* at Tiruvorraiyūr. Sometimes again the religious benefaction took the remarkable form of providing hereditary servants for temples. No. 122 of 1912 records an instance in which five women with their descendants were assigned to the temple of Tiruvorraiyūr for husking paddy. This temple, it will be noted, possessed the famous grammar-hall for teaching Pāṇini's grammar, and was a great centre of intellectual and religious activity. We have again seen instances where the religious feeling expressed itself in the rescue of images that were being removed, the reconsecration of desecrated temples, or the restoration of worship that had been neglected owing to bad times. Lastly we may instance, as further expressions of the same feeling, the foundation of *maṭhas* and monasteries which served as strongholds and centres of both religion and learning, where the higher elements of the culture of the race were conserved. Such colleges were the agencies of popular education, diffusing the light of both knowledge and religion.

Like the religious spirit the patriotism of the community also expressed itself through appropriate secular charities. We have already seen how the *smṛtis* lay down among the duties of the assemblies or *samūhas* the preservation and maintenance of public halls, wells, water-courses, and tanks for supply of water both for drink and irrigation, as also relief of the normally helpless and the occasionally helpless, in times of famine for example. Actual performances of these ideal precepts are amply recorded in our inscriptions, both North and South Indian, as we have already seen. Although the quantity of religious benefactions is much greater than that of the secular, yet we do find some remarkable examples of the latter. In the northern inscriptions, for instance, we find gifts of a cistern (*pāniyaka* and *poḍhi*) or a water-cistern (*pāṇiya-poḍhi*), benches, chairs, and walks [nos. 986, 995, 998 in Lüders's list]. But the quantity of evidence in South Indian inscriptions is, as usual, more copious. We have already considered the numerous references in the epigraphic records to the gifts of tanks, sluices, and irrigation channels, the maintenance of which was accepted by the assembly as one of its legitimate duties, for the due discharge of which a separate committee was created, called the tank committee. The tank committee, along with the garden committee, had in fact as their main duties the administration of the benefactions and trust properties which the public spirit of the community always placed at their disposal in abundance. Nor should we omit a reference to institutions like the historic grammar-hall for the teaching of Pāṇini attached to the temple of Tiruvorraiyūr, which was maintained for a long time by a serie of benefactions both private and official.

CHAPTER X

CONCLUSION

We have now completed our account of the local bodies of ancient India, their organization, structure, and functions. It is apparent that the South Indian evidence preponderates over the North Indian. The defect of the former is that it is comparatively late in dates. Nevertheless, one can trace in it the continuation of the same features and tendencies, the same principles of evolution and organization as are reflected, though dimly, in the documents of the north, both literary and epigraphic. The signal merit of the southern evidence consists in its definiteness, copiousness, and abundance of details, rendering quite explicit what is very often merely implicit in the northern, and demonstrating the practical realization in actual application of the various ideal principles and maxims of local administration embodied in our *smṛtis* and other forms of literary testimony to which we have referred in the course of this inquiry. The comparative chronological modernity of the southern evidence is indeed more than compensated by its quantity and the variety of its details which it is impossible to exhaust and investigate completely. The material is still growing, rendering the task of the investigator more arduous and his work less complete. For example, the Tanjore inscriptions alone, associated with the Chola King Rājarāja I (A. D. 985–1013), testify to the existence of no less than 150 village-assemblies and of 40 other villages where the affairs of the village were administered, as in the city-states of ancient Hellas, by all the inhabitants collectively. As Mr. Venkayya points out [*Arch. Surv. of Ind. Report* for 1904–5, p. 135] the system must have been in operation in thousands of other villages whose names and exact number await discovery by future researches. Neither the period nor the circumstances in which such village-assemblies arose in Southern India can be definitely ascertained. In Mr. Venkayya's opinion the mention by Megasthenes of six boards of five members each, to which the evidence of the Uttaramallūr inscriptions closely corresponds, favours the supposition that the system was carried into Southern India by the Aryan immigrants, and that slight alterations probably were made to suit the conditions of the south. The same hypothesis will serve to explain the lateness of date of the South Indian evidence bearing on the local bodies which seem to have owed their origin to the transplantation of the earlier North Indian institutions.

The North Indian evidence, valuable for its comparative antiquity, and its consequent anticipation of the growths reflected in the southern, is far more copious in its literary than in its epigraphic or monumental part. While the evidence as a whole is devoid of those definite and elaborate details by which we are enabled to draw a complete picture of the administrative machinery evolved and employed by local government in olden times, yet there is one unique feature in the northern material which gives us a valuable compensation for the deficiency, and serves to bring out the efficiency of the organization of these local bodies. That feature is the discovery of numerous seals and sealings issued by North Indian guilds or corporations in different localities and at various times. The earliest of these is a seal-die of terra-cotta discovered in the excavations conducted by Sir John Marshall at Bhīṭā, near Allahabad, on which he reads the legend *Śahijitiye nigamaśa*, 'written in letters of the third or perhaps fourth century B. C.' Sir John found the die at the foundation of a house which he accordingly designates as the 'House of the Guild', and remarks that 'the house in which the seal was discovered may mark the site of the office of the *nigama* or corporation' [*Arch. Surv., Annual Report*, 1911–12,

p. 47]. Four other sealings of guilds bearing the legend *nigama* or *nigamasa* inscribed in Kuṣaṇa characters have also been discovered there, together with a fifth sealing bearing the legend *nigamasya* in northern Gupta characters.

Similarly, the excavations at Basāṛh (identified with Vaiśālī) have brought to light many seals with inscriptions that connect them with the time of the Imperial Gupta kings, and 'the most numerous [class] among the seal inscriptions is that referring to the corporation or guild (*nigama*) of bankers (*śreṣṭhin*), traders (*sārttharāha*), and merchants (*kulika*). It is invariably combined with other seals, giving the names of private individuals, who were themselves traders, merchants, or bankers, and probably were the members of those guilds. One person, Hari by name, styles himself both *kulika* and *prathama kulika*, i.e. the leader of merchants. 'It looks as if during those days something like a modern chamber of commerce existed in Upper India at some big trading centre, perhaps at Pāṭaliputra' [Dr. Bloch in the *Arch. Survey, Annual Report*, 1903–4. p. 104]. The discoveries included three specimens of seals bearing the legend *śreṣṭhi-kulika-nigama*, 'the corporation of bankers (and) merchants', and no less than 274 showing the legend *śreṣṭhi-sārtthavāha-kulika-nigama* (or sometimes *nigamā*), i.e. the corporation of bankers, traders, (and) merchants. The symbol added to these merchant guilds' seals has been described by Dr. Bloch as a money-chest, because in shape it resembles the money-bag held in front from which the attendant of Lakṣmī, very probably Kubera, throws down coins, as depicted on the seals of officials. Among the names of private persons who are associated with the seals of the guilds as their members may be mentioned Ajapāla, Āryyanandi, Bhavasena, Nāgasiṁha, Dharmmo-rakṣati-rakṣita, Ghoṣa, Gomikaputtra, Ḥarigupta, Varāhasya (genitive), Iśānadāsasya (genitive), Keśavadattasya (genitive), Lakṣmaṇa, Mātridāsa, &c. We have also a number of what may be called *kulika-* and *śreṣṭhi*-seals, i. e. seals issued by *kulikas* or merchants and *śreṣṭhis* or bankers, whose names are given on them, e. g. *kulika-Dhanasya*, *śreṣṭhi-Śrīdāsasya*, &c. Again, no less than sixteen specimens of a seal bearing the legend *śreṣṭhi-nigamasya*, (seal) of the guild of bankers were discovered by the excavations of Dr. D. B. Spooner, who is thus led to make the following remark: 'Banking was evidently as prominent in Vaiśālī as we should have expected it to be, judging from the notice in Manu to the effect that the people in Magadha were bards and traders' [*Arch. Surv. Annual Report*, 1913–14, p. 122].[1]

[1] It may be interesting to note in this connexion that numerous inscribed clay seals issued by the Buddhist Saṅghas or monasteries

Besides seals and sealings the ancient Indian guilds also issued coinage, specimens of which, belonging to different periods, have been discovered in the process of archaeological exploration. On plate III of Cunningham's *Coins of Ancient India* (p. 63) are figured four coins from Taxila bearing the following obverse and reverse legends:

	Obverse	*Reverse*
No. 8	[? *T*]*ālima*[*ta*]	[*N*]*ega*[*m*]
„ 9	*Dujaka*	*Negamā*
„ 10	*Dojaka*	*Negamā*
„ 11	*A*[*taka* ?]*takā*	*Negam*[*ā*]

These coins seem to have been struck by the *negamā* or guilds of the names[1] given, and were of the nature of 'mercantile guild-tokens'. The legends on the coins are 'in beautifully formed Asokan characters, both Gandharian [Kharoṣṭhī] and Indian. Over the word *negamā* there is a single stroke or bar, as if to designate one *negamā*. On the opposite side there is a "steel-yard" very clearly represented.' These

have been discovered. Thus in the excavations near Kasia Dr. Vogel brought to light no less than 464 seals bearing the legend *śrī-Mahāparinirvāṇa-vihārē bhikṣu saṅghasya* with minor variations, which were used by the Convent of the Great Decease to seal their letters sent to another neighbouring monastery which has been traced in other nine seals. [See *Arch. Surv. Annual Report*, 1906–7, pp. 63–7.]

[1] Rapson [*J. R. A. S.*, 1900, p. 99] regards the names as those of the rulers of the guilds.

coins are partly punch-marked silver pieces and partly single or double die copper pieces, all of the standard peculiar to India, anterior to the Greek conquest of Alexander, or, more correctly, 'the Greek conquest of Demetrius'. The inscriptions are partly in Brāhmī characters of the oldest type and partly both in Brāhmī and in Kharoṣṭhī letters, which fact points to the conclusion that they are not later than the third century B. C.[1]

[1] Along with these guild-coins, we may note what Cunningham calls the 'autonomous coins of ancient India', i. e. those issued by the free clans or autonomous communities, such as the (1) *Odumbara* coins; (2) *Yaudheya* coins (with those of their chiefs Brāhmaṇa Deva and Bhānu Varma); (3) *Sibi* coins; (4) *Mālava* coins; (5) *Vaṭāśvaka* coins (probably connected with the Aśvaka tribe, the 'Assakenoi' of the Greeks, to which Rapson [*J. R. A. S.*, 1900, pp. 98–106] adds (6) *Uddehika* coins (third century B.C.); and (7) *Ārjunāyana* coins, related to the Yaudheya.

INDEX